FROM DACHAU TO D-DAY

A Memoir by Werner Kleeman

with Elizabeth Uhlig

Published by Marble House Editions
96-09 66th Avenue (Suite 1D)
Rego Park, NY 11374

Copyright © 2006 by Werner Kleeman

All rights reserved

No part of this publication may be reproduced, stored in, or introduced into a retrieval system, or transmitted in any form or by any means (electronic, mechanical, photocopying, recording or otherwise) without the prior written permission of both the copyright owner and the above publisher of this book.

Library of Congress Cataloguing-in-Publication Data

Kleeman, Werner

From Dachau to D-Day

Summary: The memoirs of a German Jew who escaped Nazi Germany, served in the American Army, and lived a long, successful and fulfilling life in the United States.

ISBN 0-9786745-3-7

Library of Congress Catalog Card Number 2006941030

This work is dedicated to my daughter,
Susan Renee Elgart,
her daughter, Allison S. Elgart,
and her son, David L. Elgart

and

my daughter, Deborah Ann Schenkein,
her daughter, Laura E. Schenkein,
and her son, Steven A. Schenkein.

Acknowledgements

To my Army Friends ~ During the 3½ years that I spent in the American Army, in both the U.S. and the European theater of operations, I met some wonderful men. These were men of special caliber, mostly middle aged, who came into the army to serve, and took pride in doing so. Some of them are named in the chapters of this book.

Since, as a group, they took an interest in me, my work and my life, this period of my life has become a special chapter. It has taught me how to respect and contribute to the welfare of the group, one that was sometimes under pressure and in danger.

The war had to be won as quickly as possible so that we could all return to our peacetime lives and join our families. To share a foxhole is a noble experience and sometimes very hard to describe, but I have tried to the best of my ability.

To my Business Friends ~ When I started my life as an independent merchant, running my little business, I started to meet and deal with architects, engineers, administrators, construction managers, and other professionals. They contributed in a wonderful way to my growth and understanding of all the business values that were needed for success. Each of the individuals imparted to me something that helped me to become a valuable person who could, in turn, help them with their business-related problems and could satisfy their special needs.

My success depended upon their input and patience to help me build the confidence needed to meet their requirements. The people in this group contributed to my success and growth during the years in which I was associated with them. They deserve a special thanks and the promise that I shall never forget them.

To my Personal Aquaintances – Please note that some names have been changed in order to protect certain parties' privacy.

To My Personal Editor and Friend, Elizabeth Uhlig –

My ability to get my thoughts on paper and portray my life as an interesting story with color and emotion would not have been possible without the assistance of my editor, Elizabeth Uhlig. Working from personal conversations, she enabled me to produce this memoir with its characteristic flair and provide a more meaningful context and description of the events of my life.

FROM DACHAU TO D-DAY

by Werner Kleeman

TABLE OF CONTENTS

Note from the Editor
Prologue
1. The Beginning: Sudden Change
2. In Custody
3. A Miracle
4. Refuge in London
5. Leaving for America
6. Drafted!
7. A Soldier in England
8. On to France
9. Belgium and Beyond
10. Back to Germany
11. Going Home
12. Family, Business and Suburban Life
13. A Respite from Work
14. A Postwar Friendship – John Groth
15. Reuniting with Old Friends
16. In Gaukönigshofen Again
17. Returning to Luxembourg
18. Enduring and Controversial Friendships
19. My Eightieth Birthday
20. Life as it is Today

Note from the Editor

It has been my supreme privilege to work with Werner Kleeman on his memoir, an oeuvre that has been long in the making.

When I first met Werner in October of 2004, he presented me with stacks of partially-written manuscripts that he had attempted to complete over the last couple of decades. Somehow, despite his earnest efforts, he had never been able to make it all gel.

I asked him to give me everything that he had written and promised to read it all and see how it could fit together. What I found was that Werner had recorded many episodes of his life multiple times, but had never addressed other pieces. Over the next two years, I would edit his work and ask him many questions in an effort to fill in the missing parts. As we worked together, more and more of Werner's life came to light. He discovered documents that had been squirreled away, bringing back memories long buried. Every time we thought we had written the last chapter of this book, another chapter of life popped up.

In addition, life kept on happening in real time. After all, Werner is not someone who has stopped participating in life and can sit back and just think about what happened. On the contrary, he is someone whose phone rings a lot, whose mailbox often contains intriguing correspondence from faraway places, and whose door frequently ushers in interesting guests. He is still living a vibrant and productive life, so when is it a good time to stop writing about it?

We decided to bring this project to a close at exactly the 2-year mark, not because it is by any means over, but rather, because we are keen to share it with you, the reader.

It is my hope that those who read this work will derive some inspiration and be uplifted by the words of someone who is truly making the most of every day.

And so, we begin....

Elizabeth Uhlig
October, 2006

PROLOGUE

Writing one's memoirs is a curious process. It requires a review of an entire life and a willingness to look at the parts of it that seem to be the most salient, the most significant.

A memoir is not a biography but rather, a kind of verbal photo album in which the most cherished and dramatic moments or episodes are preserved. As an older American, now living comfortably in my home in Queens, New York, where I have lived for decades and raised my two daughters, I can reflect upon the many chapters of my life that have come before this period. I gaze at these various events of my personal history and delight in remembering not so much what happened, but what kinds of meaningful friendships and relationships developed through my experiences. I enjoy thinking about the people who were not permanent fixtures in my life, but who were more like characters who have passed through it.

Although only temporary presences in my long life, these people have had a tremendous impact on the way I view the world and my own value in it. When I think about all that has happened thus far, certain "characters" come up as having played pivotal roles in the drama that is my story.

1. THE BEGINNING: SUDDEN CHANGE

The tale I want to share begins not during my childhood, but in my late teens, when the rumblings of the Third Reich were having more and more of a terrifying and disastrous effect on those of us living in middle Europe.

Although this is not a Holocaust memoir, some of it does take place during WWII and bears witness to some of the horrors of the Nazi regime, my memoir reaches beyond the boundaries of wartime into the smaller, more intimate moments, when life seemed its most precious.

I shall begin in 1939, when I was a young man of 19, growing up in a small village in Germany, Gaukönigshofen. Until 1934, life had been very peaceful. We Jews, who had been in this part of Europe for centuries, led our lives in the community without conflict. Our village was one of well-to-do farmers' homes, and the earth around the village was blessed with rich soil which always yielded good crops. This small, independent village of 600 people was considered to be one of the best breadbaskets of Germany.

My father was a grain merchant and my parents, my three brothers, my sister and I comprised a middle class, rather religious family. My father was respected in the community and his wisdom in business was later to exert a strong influence on me. He counted every penny and managed the family business without loans from the bank. And more important, he was impeccable in his integrity.

He had fought in WWI, and a photo in my collection shows him in a proud pose. A slim young man with a dark moustache, he wears a uniform and cap, and stands with one hand behind his back and the other in front, holding a cigar. He looks every bit the European soldier – serious and dignified.

Our home was dignified as well. We lived in one of the more palatial ones in that part of Germany. Our house was built in the early 1700s and had belonged to a wealthy burgher, and it had somehow come into my family's possession.

The structure itself was an imposing, well balanced architectural masterpiece with a sloping roof and thick walls. The facade was painted a pale yellow. It was built like an old fortress and was luxurious, but had no running water. I remember when, in 1929, we had running water put in. This was a rather novel idea, and an amenity only in the homes of well-to-do families. A house such as ours was coveted by many, and

we felt lucky to be living there. We did not know then that we would be the last family of Jews to occupy it.

The photo, of course, does not do the house justice. It reveals only a shadow of the house's original majesty. How sad and dull it looks, but this is appropriate, because once we left that house, whatever dignity it had once had vanished forever.

My mother was not from Gaukönigshofen, but from the neighboring village of Wiesenfeld. She had been introduced to my father by the wife of the local Hebrew school teacher. The teacher's wife had met my maternal grandmother one day in Würzburg, where both women were shopping. Würzburg was the closest large city, and if one wanted to buy anything substantial, a trip into "town" was necessary. When the two women ran into each other that day, the teacher's wife, who knew my father and his family, suggested a match for my grandmother's daughter. The ensuing marriage brought my mother to the village where she, my father, and the rest of us would live until Germany became an unlivable place.

Daily life in Gaukönigshofen was such that everyone knew everyone else. Jews and non-Jews appeared to respect one another, which was a good thing, because the village was 99% Catholic. It was a very traditional little village, replete with folk arts, including the colorful, elaborate costumes that women wore to church on Sunday. Like a lot of prewar German villages, Gaukönigshofen seemed to display that romantic innocence that poets and artists have portrayed in their work.

The village itself had some of the best examples of Baroque and Rococo architecture in Germany, and village scenes resembled illustrations from German fairy tales. There were residential and commercial buildings with gabled rooves, churches with onion-shaped domes and delicate steeples, and facades in pale colors. There was a poetic stillness to the cobbled pathways, red-orange tiles, tranquil brooks that offered reflections of the graceful trees. A town crest dating from 1724 crowned the entryway to one of the town's finest buildings, lending a certain air of dignity to such a small village. But this tranquility and quaintness was soon to be broken.

We were five children – four boys and my sister Ruth, who was the youngest. A photo taken around 1926 shows all of us in our best clothes, standing in a rather relaxed but still formal group. The boys are wearing ensembles resembling uniforms, complete with military-style caps. Ruth is wearing a tiny, dark dress and atop her head sits an enormous bow. We look well groomed, well fed, and certainly well loved. And for a time, this was an honest representation of our life.

Being German, we led somewhat regimented lives, adhering to all the rules of the school system, obeying the law, not asking questions. I think now, though, that we lived under the false

illusion that life was going to continue peacefully. As far back as 1936, we had seen the rising tide of Nazi persecution. All over Europe, Jews' rights and privileges were being eroded by the Third

Reich. This started as small deprivations of personal liberties and went on to grow into a mass acceptance of the idea that Jews could not have anything of their own.

For me, the trouble started when I was thrown out of school at age 14. Then came the "Aryanization" of Jewish businesses, in which non-Jewish "managers" were placed on staff in companies and shops. It was not long before entire businesses were confiscated and boycotted, and Aryan citizens were forbidden to do business with Jews.

Then came the more public announcements: no Jews in cafés, theatres, universities, hotels, tramways, public toilets, not even on park benches! Our housekeeper, Elisabeth, who had been a member of our household for about five or six years, had to be let go because of a law stating that Christians could not be employed by Jews. She was forced to leave my mother with the entire responsibility of all the cooking, cleaning and shopping for a household with five children.

As we saw what was happening and how it was affecting our private and public lives, we applied for visas to get out of Germany. That was not easy, because it was as if all the doors had closed. One of my brothers had the foresight to leave Germany back in 1936 when he saw the trend of increasingly outward displays of anti-Semitism. As the first family member to apply, he was the first to obtain a visa. All that the rest of us could do was wait, with no way of knowing anything, since Jews were not allowed to own radios.

On November 9, 1938, my oldest brother was summoned to come to the American Consulate in Stuttgart to get his visa to immigrate to the United States. His plan was to get the visa and passport and go through Basel, Switzerland. His timing was great, because November 9th was what was henceforth known as *Kristallnacht*, the "Night of Broken Glass," which gravely affected Jews all over Europe.

Kristallnacht was the Nazis' way of retaliating for the murder of a German diplomat, which had taken place in Paris. When a certain Jewish man in Paris walked into the German consulate, he had but one mission: to kill any official facing him. His parents had been expelled from Germany and had also been refused entrance into Poland, their home state. Little did this man know or realize that the Nazis would use this incident as a stepping stone to launch an offensive across Germany against all Jews.

On that November night, an order, or something more like *carte blanche*, was given to all non-Jews to destroy synagogues, Jewish businesses and homes everywhere, and little encouragement was needed for ordinary citizens to take part in the effort.

Kristallnacht was a free-for-all of vandalism. Word was sent out that anyone could go out and beat up Jews and destroy, plunder and steal from all Jewish businesses and homes.

Of course, we had known that the Nazi regime was ready to arrest and destroy all Jews, but we could never have imagined the magnitude of their plan. The lowest ranking members of society and the most uneducated ones were called upon to participate in this spontaneous destruction of human values, lives and property. These criminals put on their official uniforms to make it look like an ordered method of vandalism. The blueprint went out that all male Jews were to be arrested and put into concentration camps, which had been readied for this purpose. There was no warning signal, just the beginning of acts of destruction. There was no police action to stop these wild gangsters and no one stood in their way. It was as though it had been secretly planned and was just waiting for the right moment to burst open. And it did – all across Germany, with the exception of a few small counties that were not notified and were miraculously left out of the plan.

A few incidents had already occurred before the effects of *Kristallnacht* reached us personally. The "job" started when a group of thugs arrived in Ochsenfuhrt. Apparently, they had had time to prepare and organize themselves. They had requested a truck from a building supply tradesman in the hope of using it to load Jews and take them to jail, thus preventing them from hiding or running away. When the tradesman refused to lend them his vehicle, they went after a corn dealer who had a truck. He consented, and became an accomplice to the Nazi terror.

The thugs planned to leave after dark from a restaurant in Frühlingstrasse. Meanwhile, word leaked out and people began to arm themselves with heavy wooden sticks, which they would use for beating Jews and corralling them into the truck. A man from my village, who worked in Ochsenfuhrt, heard all about this and telephoned some of the Jews in the village to warn them about the planned violence.

My brother knew he was leaving Germany for good that night. We had driven in our family car for four hours to Stuttgart so that he could go to the American consulate there. At about 5 PM, he left the building, now equipped with his passport and the visa for the U.S. He was ready to leave for Switzerland, and I was planning to drive back home.

In Stuttgart, innkeepers were clearing out hotels and advising people to leave. As I stood there, I watched incredulously as hoodlums destroyed the Jewish businesses around the hotel. Filled with anxiety, I left the city immediately and started to drive home. By 9PM, I had reached Bad Mergentheim and called home from a public phone to see what was going on in the village. My father said, "You'd better not come now, the Nazis are on their way." As I tried to hold this brief conversation, in the background I could hear people screaming, saying that the synagogue in

Bad Mergentheim, which was about 15 miles from my village, was burning and that the vicious mobs were going wild.

I drove another 15 kilometers to Euerhausen, to the home of a farmer I knew well, and asked him if I could spend the night. He agreed to this, but asked that, for my safety as well as his, I leave at 5AM. He did not trust his own servants' discretion, for this was a time in which life had become so perverse that denouncing the next person was considered a virtue. Since cars were still rather rare for private citizens, my car outside the farmer's house would be a dead giveaway, an obvious clue that a stranger was spending the night. So before daybreak, I left and drove to Wolkshausen and checked in with another farmer. He let me stay until 7AM, at which time I left and headed home.

When I got to Gaukönigshofen, I found our home completely devastated. The front door had been forced open and dismantled. Every window was smashed, every wooden closet and cupboard, as well as their contents – porcelain and glass — were destroyed. All the bedding had been sliced open….nothing had been spared the violent assault.

In fact, all the Jewish houses were destroyed that night and all the Jewish men were taken away to prison. The nightmare of it all was that the villagers themselves participated in this destruction. These were people I had known very well, some of whom made their living from my father! They were fanatic, they were brainwashed, believing that cooperating and collaborating with the Nazi regime was somehow going to improve their lives. Up to about a few months before that, it seemed that they had not even known what it meant to hate a Jew. This was part of the illusion that we were living.

Of course, the seeds of anti-Semitism had always been present in middle Europe. They just needed the right circumstances in which to blossom, if such a lovely word can be used to explain this piece of history.

In the middle of this destruction, I was thinking about how I had grown up with these people, gone to school with them, worked with them. We were all on a first name basis with each other. Some of them were friends, some business acquaintances.

Some of these neighbors' sons and farmers' sons

had been working for about 25 years for my father, hauling corn every week from the warehouse to the railroad station or the mill. They had made good money from their employment, but overnight, they had turned into Nazi accomplices. I recognized the faces of the people involved in the devastation of our way of life, people who were good Catholics who went to church every morning and twice on Sundays. We just could not believe that this was happening.

During the night the looting continued. The villagers took cattle from the cattle dealers, leading them home to their own property. They tied up the animals and simply claimed them for their own. In fact, they took everything that was not nailed down.

It was frightening to see this happen so quickly, literally from one day to the next. All at once, it was as though we were surrounded by a new type of people, and as though, unbeknownst to us, there was an energy residing in them, an energy that had suddenly been released and had gone wild. Perhaps they themselves did not know they had it in them. They suddenly began to rejoice - at last, they were able to do something to the Jews!

The next morning we learned that all the men of our village had been taken away during the night and no one knew where they were. It did not take long before I, too, was arrested by a Nazi party official and taken to the office of the local gendarme. They were happy to arrest us, to finally be rid of this scourge on their territory. People have asked why I did not try to run away that night, but I knew then that it was only a matter of time before they'd catch up with me, especially since I had a car. There was really no place to hide.

But we did not even know the complete story....I later learned what had happened during the night and I could now understand the velocity of the destruction and the treatment of the Jews during the night. Two farmers, well known to us, kept a bonfire going outside the synagogue. They ripped out all the pews, the Torah scrolls, and the ark that held the scrolls, and threw them into the fire, keeping it going until morning. Mercifully, the local fire marshal did not permit them to burn down the building itself, because he was afraid the entire village would go up in flames. The population was watching and stimulating the violence....

They had kicked the local school teacher, took people away barefoot, not even giving them time to get dressed. They rounded them up in the village square and had trucks come to take them away. And in the end, we learned that on *Kristallnacht*, 30,000 Jewish men throughout Germany had been sent away.

2. IN CUSTODY

When I was arrested, I was taken to the jail at Ochsenfurt, where I was put in a cell with my father. He did not even know that my brother had left Germany for Switzerland. When I told him, he was glad to learn that at least one of us had gotten out, because all male Jews from the surrounding villages in the district had been thrown in prison.

Our routine as prisoners was soon established. We were not allowed to talk to anyone, and had to stay in the cell, with the exception of a 15-minute walk around the courtyard during the afternoon. We could not say a word. We did not know what was going on or what would happen next, but we did know that a few of the detainees had been very badly beaten and bruised, such that they had to be sent to the local hospital. We were cut off from the rest of the world with no communication. And we were not allowed to ask any questions.

After a week or so in prison, my father and a few other old men were released on the strength of their having been WWI German army veterans. The rest of us were told that we were being moved to Würzburg, where there was a larger prison.

We were in the new location about two weeks before we were preparing for another move to somewhere unknown. The Gestapo took over and made all the preparations. We were transported in a convoy of about five buses to Dachau, which was famous for its concentration camp. Others of our community were sent to Buchenwald, an equally odious place.

We trundled along in broken down buses, accompanied by lots of policemen. On the six-hour trip, there was no comfort whatsoever, no food, water or bathroom facilities. We made the trip in total silence. The only comfort was in knowing that my mother and father were at home and not with us.

Upon arrival in Dachau, we were processed as prisoners who could not even think, much less ask what our fate would be. Dachau was really just a holding area when I went there, but it grew to be famous, along with the other concentration camps, because of the extermination program that was eventually carried out there.

For new arrivals, first there was a haircut, followed by a change from clothes into prison outfits, which were a kind of a lightweight, striped pajama and ill-fitting shoes. Our own clothes were shoved into bags and stored in a locked closet, to ensure that no one would run away. The Germans had a well thought-out system for everything.

Then came the assignment of barracks, where we would sleep on hard wooden slats, with thin, itchy blankets that offered little warmth. All of the orientation work was done by other prisoners who had passed through these channels before us.

The first morning there was the call out for *appel*, (roll call) and that was how every day began. The *appel* could last for hours, and one simply had to stand and be present. If they wanted us to stand outside for 18 hours, we did it, day or night.

Somehow, perhaps fortunately, I do not completely recall how the rest of the day was spent. There was nothing to do - no work for

30,000 people! We stood there in our pajamas, 10, 12 hours a day, depending on what mood our captors were in. The German November was cold, and we had minimal food, perhaps a cup of soup each day. There were no questions or explanations whatsoever. In fact, there was not even anyone to ask, because the SS guards would not speak to us.

We saw people getting killed on the electrified fence every day, and we saw others starving, sick and dying. About 10-12 people died every day, some from beating, some from having been torn to shreds by vicious dogs, and some from starvation.

There were corpses piled up and taken for burial every morning, or perhaps they were shipped home. We did not know, we did not ask, and we did not think. We just existed. No one I knew personally died while I was there but in a sense, everyone was a personal friend because we were all part of one, large suffering body.

Somewhere among the 30,000 prisoners were two of my cousins, and although I rarely saw them, there was some kind of comfort in knowing that they were there. Of course, Jewish communities in prewar Europe were often composed of extended families, so it would not be unusual for family members to find themselves living close to one another. But in this case, we were sharing the same concentration camp.

Also in the camp was Bernard Weikersheimer, a fellow from my village. I became aware of his presence one day when I heard his name over the loudspeaker. He was being summoned to the commandant's office.

Bernard Weikersheimer was a cattle merchant who was picked up by the SS while doing business at the cattle market in Augsburg. In those days, a Jew could be plucked out of daily life at any time and sent away immediately, with no possibility of contacting people at home.

When I met up with Bernard later, he told me what had happened on the day he was summoned to the office. The commandant on duty was a Captain Greenwald, who came from Frickenhausen, a village near where Bernard had come from. (It was most unusual for a camp commandant to come from a small village. They were usually city-bred people.)

The commandant knew that Bernard had a car,

and offered to buy it from him at a very low price. This was his way of telling Bernard that he would lose his vehicle one way or the other, so he might as well sell it to him. Because Bernard did not get out of Dachau when I did, I never got to hear the results of this deal-making, but it was so typical of the way life was for us.

Everything we owned could simply be appropriated by the German government, no questions asked. We had no rights at all and nothing of ours was sacred to them. I remember that during the early stages of the Nazi takeover, around 1933, my father got a call from someone in the government. He was told that his car, a Mercedes, would be taken, as it was needed for "party business." About two weeks after the car was appropriated, my father got a call saying that the car had been in an accident. The wreck could be picked up in Karlstadt, which was about 20 miles away. My father sent the dealer to inspect the damage, and as it turned out, the car had been totally destroyed. It was a complete loss for which my father never received any compensation.

3. A MIRACLE

I always say that I was one of the lucky ones. I was allowed to get out of Dachau on the condition that I was going to leave Germany, and I intended to leave right away. Why would I not want to leave? It is amazing to me that some people did not feel the pressure to get out of Germany, as I did, after *Kristallnacht*.

This photo, taken shortly after my release from Dachau, does not convey to the unsuspecting spectator anything about what I had been through. But a fellow inmate would recognize the very short haircut that was emblematic of the status of a prisoner!

The background on my efforts to get out of Germany is one of those astonishing Holocaust stories. Before the actual, tangible trouble had begun, I had written to a second cousin in the U.S., whose name I had gotten from a first cousin. This person, who was eventually my sponsor,

lived in Nebraska. I never got to meet him, but he saved my life because at that time, you could not set anything in motion if you did not have a U.S. citizen to vouch for you.

One day I was notified by a bank that a letter of credit for $5,000 had been put on deposit for me from this distant relative. I obtained an affidavit for this and my mother sent it to the consulate in Stuttgart, who then transferred it to London.

The British government sent the letter to Frankfurt and I was released on December 22nd. The Jewish community of Munich received me and arranged for transportation from Dachau back home. With the way things were progressing in Germany, this kind of courtesy was not to last for long. Here are the contents of the letter:

British Consulate General
62, Guiollettestrasse
Frankfurt a. Main
Ref. NO 26/5/3995 – 38

December 9, 1938

This is to inform you that you will receive a visa to enter England as soon as you present a passport at this office.

This confirmation is issued in duplicate. One form is to be presented to the Gestapo for your release from the concentration camp.

The other copy is to be used to apply for a passport at the passport office.

This confirmation is good for:

Mr. Werner Kleemann, and wife

residing at Gaukönigshofen, near Würzburg a. Main

Royal British Consul General

* * * * * * * *

British Consulate General,
68, Guiollettstrasse
Frankfurt a. Main

Ref No.
26/5/3995 -38

den, 9. Dezember 1938

Zum Zwecke der Vorlage bei den zuständigen deutschen Behörden bestätige ich hiermit, dass ich bereit bin Ihnen ein Sichtvermerk zur Einreise nach England zu erteilen, sobald Sie im Besitze eines gültigen Reisepasses sind.

Diese Bescheinigung wird für Häftlinge in doppelter Ausführung ausgestellt. Ein Exemplar ist mit dem Haftentlassungsantrag der Geheimen Staatspolizei einzureichen. Das andere Exemplar ist mit dem Passantrag an die zuständige Stelle einzureichen, welche Reisepässe ausstellt.

Diese Bescheinigung ist gültig für:

Herrn Werner Kleemann, und Ehefrau
Gaukönigshofen b. Würzburg a. Main

Kgl.Grossbrit. Generalkonsul

I arrived home at 7:30 the next morning, thrilled to find my parents, sister and brother there. I immediately started preparations for my emigration from Germany, and getting a passport was my top priority. I applied to the British consulate and within only two weeks, I was issued a visa to enter Great Britain. I felt that I could not get out of Germany soon enough.

There was one more piece of paper I needed in order to "buy" my freedom: the *Certificate of Good Behavior*, issued on January 16, 1939.

A rather Spartan document, it simply states that it is all right for me to leave, that I have no offenses against me. I use the word "buy" because I did have to pay the German government 2,000 German marks in order to leave. This would be about $500 in today's currency. The paper verifying this is dated January 11, 1939, only days before I got my *Certificate of Good Behavior*.

It was a small price to pay for my life. However, it is still amazing to me that I was able to organize all of these papers in time to get out, and that I did, in fact, leave Germany unharmed. And when I left, I thought, as *of this moment, I am no longer a German. I am starting a new life.*

Ochsenfurt, den 16. Januar 1939.

Führungszeugnis.

~~zum Zwecke~~ Gültig für Auswanderungszwecke und gültig für drei Monate, vom Tage der Ausstellung an gerechnet.

Herr — ~~Frau~~ — ~~Frl.~~ Werner Israel K l e e m a n n

geboren am 26. September 1919 in Gaukönigshofen

~~ist~~ hier ~~seit~~
war   vom 26. März 1937   bis 12. Januar 1939

in Gaukönigshofen

polizeilich gemeldet.

Auf Grund der hier geführten polizeilichen Strafliften (Polizeiakten) sind im polizeilichen Führungszeugnis

keine
~~folgende~~ Strafen oder sonstigen Vermerke zu verzeichnen.

J.A.

(Stempel)   (Unterschrift)

Gebühr:
Verz. Nr.

Der Oberfinanzpräsident Würzburg　　　　　Würzburg, 11.1.1939
　　- Devisenstelle -　　　　　　　　　　Ludwigstr. 8/II, Telefon 2502
Nr. Dev. 2196 Ho/F

Zum Schreiben vom -　　　　　Herrn

　　　　　　　　　　　　　　　　Werner Israel Kleemann,

　　　　　　　　　　　　　　　　　　　Gaukönigshofen.

Betr.: Umzugsgut.

　　　　　　Ich vermag die Mitnahme des Umzugsgutes

　　　nach USA

nur dann zu genehmigen, wenn eine unentgeltliche Abgabe von
RM 2ooo.-- (Reichsmark zweitausend), worin eine Busse von
RM 5oo.-- wegen falschen Angaben enthalten ist,
an die Deutsche Golddiskontbank, Berlin C 111, entrichtet
wird.

　　　　　　Anhand des Bankbeleges ersuche ich mir die Über-
weisung nachzuweisen.

　　　　　　　　　　　　　　　　　　Im Auftrage:

4. REFUGE IN LONDON

As a refugee, I knew how lucky I was, but I also knew that I would not be safe until I crossed the German border. My mother helped me prepare for the journey. I took some clothes and little else, knowing that at the railroad station the chief of the Gestapo would search me thoroughly to make sure I was not taking anything of value.

My passport, which I still have, has a gloomy green cover and the ever bone-chilling eagle and swastika, the symbol of the Third Reich. Inside, a large red "J" sits in the upper left hand corner, and my name, written in a rather quaint looking script, reads "*Kleemann, Werner Israel.*" The Nazis gave all Jewish men the middle name "Israel," as one more way to segregate us from the rest of the German population.

The black and white photo shows a callow young man with hopeful eyes and a not so subtle smile. I don't know if this was because of my naturally

optimistic nature or if I was just happily anticipating getting out of an ever worsening set of circumstances.

It was painful to leave my family behind, but somehow I knew I would get them out of Germany too. On January 10, 1939, I left for England, a new but temporary terrain. My father stood with me on the station platform as we awaited the train in Würzburg. I could see that he was happy to watch me leave Germany and get out of danger.

The train left at 12 noon, destined for Hook of Holland, where I would catch the ferry. It was about a six-hour ride, followed by a two-hour wait at the border. I remember that the train was filled with a variety of passengers. Not everyone was on an escape mission, as I was. Some people were just going about their lives, seemingly as if nothing extraordinary were going on in Europe. There was a young, rather glamorous woman in the compartment with me, carrying her skis. She was casually returning from a ski trip to

Switzerland, and seemed not to have a care in the world, in contrast to me, a fleeing Jew.

By the time we reached Holland, it was dusk, and by the time we boarded the ship, it was dark. The Channel crossing took five hours, and because of the pitch darkness, I could not see the ocean. Having grown up in a landlocked part of Germany, I had never seen the ocean before, so crossing the Channel should have been a thrilling experience, but the truth is that the real thrill was simply going toward freedom and safety.

Upon my arrival in London, a cousin picked me up at the station. It was so good to feel free! He delivered me to one of London's kosher boarding houses, in the North end of the city, where he had paid in advance for a two-week stay for me. These are the types of acts of kindness people performed in such terrible times, and such benevolence you can never repay, but can only offer to others along the way.

I started to acquaint myself with London life and began visiting relatives, seeking help to rescue my parents, brother and sister, so that they too could leave Germany. Then a twist of fate offered me the solution I was seeking. At the boarding house there was a weekly card game. One night, one of the players, having heard my name, asked for me. He introduced himself as Norbert Lehman and I soon learned that his father and mine had been very good friends. They both came from a little village called Theilhein where, in fact, my father was born. Norbert Lehman turned out to be my mentor and savior.

Norbert was a 35-year old diamond dealer who had his own office in the Diamond Center in London. He had already been in England for quite a few years, and by the time I met him, he had become a well known diamond merchant. He took me into his home and showed me around the business. He bought me lunch, and we became good friends. Knowing I was in a fix, he offered to help me get my family out of Germany, to England.

It was miraculous! Within a week, Norbert arranged for me to get a letter offering employment to my brother and sister so that they could come to London. Now we just had to wait for the work permits to come through. Norbert also had his aunt sign an affidavit for my parents…. something my own relatives would not do. These relatives did not give a reason, but I have always assumed they simply did not want to get involved.

```
TELEGRAMS:                              46, 47, 48, 49, REDCROSS STREET
KLEEMABRO, LONDON
   TELEPHONE:         N/GB.                        LONDON E.C.1.
NATIONAL 5341, 2 & 3
      3211                                     13th DECEMBER, 1939.
```

Dear Mr. Kleemann,

     We are in receipt of your letter of the 12th instant and are somewhat surprised at your demand especially as you had mentioned to us that you had given instructions to the Anglo Palestine Bank, in London, to refund the money which your Son had sent you from Palestine.

     Under the circumstances we are afraid we are not in a position to help you.

     Yours truly,

Mr. Kleemann,
74 Finsbury Park Road,
N.4.

The letter speaks for itself, with its cold and distant tone.

None of this mattered though, because out of nowhere, my problems were suddenly solved by Norbert Lehman! I can only imagine what my family's fate would have been were it not for Norbert's good deeds. Very few families had the luck that I had, to save my immediate family from the ovens and gas chambers.

My parents came over first, and I remember the day they arrived in London. It was an April morning and the sun was shining. I went alone to get them at the Liverpool Street Station, the same station where I had come into London.

It was a moment that is hard to describe. I had been waiting for them for two long, tense months, only communicating through the mail. Now we would be together, and we suddenly knew that we would be free, united and free, and happily anticipating my brother and sister joining us before long.

The three of us got into a taxi and went to my apartment, where we would live for the next year. Knowing I would have to put my family somewhere, I had used some of the money my brother in Israel sent me to rent a furnished apartment at 74 Finsbury Park Road. It was in a quiet neighborhood of small houses. I believe that this house, which bore witness to a very important year of our lives, is still standing today.

The apartment was comprised of three rooms and a kitchen on the second floor of a one-family house. At that time, it cost about 30 shillings a week, which today would be about $15 a week. It had some of the quaint, now inconvenient, amenities that prewar European apartments are known for, like the little gas meter in which you'd put a shilling to get a few hours' worth of gas.

We got settled there and about one week later, we made a brisket dinner in honor of our hero, Mr. Lehman. We wanted him to know that we were most grateful for his kindness. He stayed humble and told us that he had done what he did because of the old friendship between our fathers.

As our own friendship continued, I would see him when I would go into the city. Or on Saturdays, I would go out to his home on the outskirts of London. He was always very warm, very kind.

* * * * * * * *

I had to find work and, having learned English back in high school in Germany, I was able to land a little clerical job in London. It "officially" was a volunteer position because it was illegal for me to work, since I had no work visa. I did, however, get paid something under the table for this little job. This was essential because I had to pay my living expenses and those of my family.

The job was in an agency for Jewish immigrants called The Bloomsbury House. I worked for a lawyer who was very well connected, and my task was to help with the immigration process, especially when there were problems. The beauty of this work was that it allowed me to utilize the agency's network of acquaintances to further the cause of getting my sister and brother their work visas.

* * * * * * * *

When I think back on this time period, I am still haunted by what I consider to be a failure in my own judgment. There was a family I could have helped, and didn't, not because I did not want to, but because I did not have the awareness.

This episode in my story takes me back to the early 1930s, when I was in high school in Würzburg. I used to sit on the school bench with a classmate named Ernest Seligsberger. Although our backgrounds were different – I came from a strict Orthodox family and he from a very liberal Jewish family – we became good friends.

Ernest was the only son of an illustrious family of art collectors. They owned and operated the third largest antique furniture store in Germany, and they lived in the beautiful apartment above the store. They dealt with England's royal family, among many other wealthy clients.

When Hitler came to power in 1933, Ernest's father sent him away to school in Switzerland, where he trained to be a physical education teacher. When he finished his studies, he went to Holland, where his family had a gallery with some of the world's most famous paintings. It was during my time in London that Ernest was in Holland, and I wonder still to this day, why I did not write him and ask how I could help him get out of there. Of course, we never anticipated that Holland would be overrun by Nazis and that its Jews would be deported and murdered. I do regret this failure, and it still haunts me as I write......

The Seligsbergers sold their store and the family was then brought back to Berlin, where they were last seen cleaning streets for the Nazis. That was the end of them, for they were taken away on one of the transports. Just three family members managed to get away: one niece went to Israel, another went to Canada, and a nephew went to New York. One of the nieces had a memorial plaque installed at the Jewish cemetery in Würzburg, in the family's honor.

Herman Göring was photographed leaving the gallery in Holland, where he selected 875 paintings for his different homes. Of course, his art collection was made up of confiscated and stolen goods. This was later splashed on the front page of The New York Times, only to bring more pain to those of us acquainted with the Seligsbergers. Some of these paintings are now housed in museums around the world.

There is more sadness still: in 1945, during the Royal Air Force's attack on Würzburg, the building that once housed the furniture store burned to the ground, and now there is nothing on that site. So much loss took place, and I indirectly played a role in it. If only I had helped that boy to get out of Holland! At least I could have saved a small piece of the family. To mitigate my pain, I have had a commemorative stone placed in the sidewalk at the site of the former Seligsberger furniture store. I felt that this was something I could do to honor the family.

* * * * * * * *

But my family was lucky, because a few months after my parents came to London, my brother and sister finally arrived too. We had another glorious reunion. Now we were together once again! With their work permits, my brother and sister quickly found ways to earn money. My brother learned carpentry and my sister did domestic work in other people's houses. My parents, of course, were not permitted to work, so during the day they walked around London. They did not speak English, so they could not even go to the movies. They passed the time talking with other German Jewish refugees.

With my little job, I was able to help my friend Bernard Weikersheimer, who had been with me in Dachau, to get out of Germany. I had brought his papers to the lawyer I worked for, and after a short time, Bernard arrived in London with his mother. They stayed in a house across the street, but ultimately left and went to America. Many other people arrived from Germany as well, and we all lived together in that neighborhood in North London. It was a rather tight-knit group, as many other refugees were living in the same circumstances.

We had no English friends, but made friends, instead, with some girls who came from Würzburg. Since there was no money to spend on amusement, we used to go to Hyde Park and pass whatever leisure time we had listening to people give speeches. Slowly, life began to seem a little more normal. We were free, breathing free air. But we knew what was going on in Europe because I was able to read the newspaper and listen to the radio. And that is how we learned that on September 1, 1939, war had been declared.

I remember the wave of emotion when we heard that Germany had attacked Poland. The first air raid went off at noon, engendering a lot of panic and frenzy all around London. And on September 3, Britain and France declared war on Germany.

5. LEAVING FOR AMERICA

The war had been on for four months when my visa to travel to the United States came through. I got a call from the American consulate and, although I was exhilarated, I also felt fear and anxiety. Again, I was extremely fortunate because although I might have been sent to Central America or Australia, I was destined to end up in the U.S. Once again, I was stepping into the unknown, without my family.

Now I would be permitted to leave, but although I had a visa, I had no money for a ticket. I had purchased a ship ticket back in Germany, but with the war going on, of course this ticket was now obsolete. I had to go around asking friends to help me buy my passage to America, and little by little, I got together the fare, which amounted to 30 pounds. Today this would be about $120, which was certainly the *cheapest* possible ticket!

At the end of November, I departed from the port

at Liverpool. I had the most Spartan accommodation, way down in the lower deck of what was probably the oldest and slowest boat. There were no luxuries, and the ship was rather empty and completely dark, since the world was at war. Passengers were not allowed to go on deck and we only hoped that the German submarines wouldn't find us.

After about 12 dark and dangerous days of travel, we did get safely to the U.S, landing at dock No. 50 in New York. It was 11AM on a clear, sunny day, and there was the city, glorious and majestic on this December morning. At that moment, I thought, *Here I am*. It was good to be in a new, different world, America, the land of liberty, of freedom. Only someone who has had to flee their homeland in search of peace and safety can fully appreciate this feeling.

With the debacle that had taken place in Germany, I felt that I had left nothing behind. All I cared about was my family, who, I hoped, would come a month or two later when their visas came through. Now I knew that I would be able to settle in, to work, I could speak out with no fear of oppression. I would have a new beginning.

I got off the boat with my two suitcases, and after some trouble getting from the dock to the subway at 42nd Street, I made my way to some cousins' house in Jackson Heights, a middle class neighborhood in Queens. My cousins, Paula and Sigmund Hopfenmeier, and their 10-year old daughter Margot, had come to New York a couple of years earlier and had a lovely apartment, filled with all their possessions. They had beautiful furniture, antiques that they had brought over from Europe. They had been quite wealthy in Europe, where they had owned a successful business importing toys into Germany from Japan and Czechoslovakia. But all that was history now.

I had arrived in New York with about $2.50 in my pocket (today's equivalent would be about $10). Since I had my green card, I immediately went to the city to look for work, and was willing to take anything that was available. My first impression of life in New York was that everything looked so different. It looked nothing like the world I had known — Germany and England. It seemed as though everyone was working, rushing off somewhere, running to their jobs in the morning and dashing home at night.

Being a refugee in New York, a Jewish boy right out of Europe, I looked different. One could always tell who the foreigners were, even as they observed us walking in the street. We had no money to buy American clothes, so we wore our less stylish European clothes, as well as noticeably different hats and shoes. Yes, you could tell who was born in America and who was not.

It took me two days of walking up and down the busy streets of Manhattan, along Broadway toward downtown, to find a position as a stock boy at S. Klein, the department store in Union Square. I used to work from 8AM to 6PM, and I got paid $12 a week, in cash. From that I had to pay my cousin $8.00 a week for room and board. The other $4.00 went for subway fare, food and a haircut. But I soon improved my situation. After six months at S. Klein, I landed a job as a salesman at Charm Sportswear, a line of ladies' clothing. It paid fifteen dollars a week and in those days, a three dollar increase in salary made a big difference.

Meanwhile, my family got the visas and came to New York. Once again, I picked them up at the boat, as I had in London. Curiously, they came over on the same boat I had come on two months earlier! We all went to Jackson Heights, but only for the weekend, because their ultimate destination was Baltimore.

During my time in New York, I visited Norbert Lehman's brother and parents, whom I had known back in Germany. (They had come to the U.S. before the war started.) I always felt that I wanted to keep up my connection with them, as Norbert had been instrumental in the determining the course of my life and that of my family. He was an extraordinary man, and his generosity played the most important role in my fate.

6. DRAFTED

On December 7, 1941, the Japanese bombed Pearl Harbor, and war was declared on Germany. The world was like a fireball. America began to prepare for an all-out war. Germany was victorious in Holland, where the Germans had dropped into Rotterdam in the middle of the night. They drank in the glory as France, the Netherlands, Belgium and Luxembourg collapsed. The Continent was in German hands.

Now all young Americans had the chance to show our support. I would have volunteered, but a non-citizen might be suspected of being a spy if they did that, so I had to wait to be called. Sure enough, in August, 1942, I got a letter saying "You have been selected…." And from there, everything happened very quickly.

When I reported to the local draft board, I did not know that I would be giving almost the next four years of my life to my newly accepted country. I,

Prepare in Triplicate

```
Local Board ... 265      25
Queens County            681
                         256
37-13 82nd Street
  (SEAT OF LOCAL BOARD)
Jackson Heights
```

July 22, 1942.
(Date of mailing)

ORDER TO REPORT FOR INDUCTION

The President of the United States,

To ____Werner_____Kleeman_____
      (First name)   (Middle name)   (Last name)

Order No. __3647__

GREETING:

Having submitted yourself to a Local Board composed of your neighbors for the purpose of determining your availability for training and service in the armed forces of the United States, you are hereby notified that you have now been selected for training and service in the ____Army____
(Army, Navy, Marine Corps)

You will, therefore, report to the Local Board named above at __3713 - 82nd Street, Jackson Heights, New York__,
(Place of reporting)

at __7 A.__ m., on the __10th__ day of __August__, 19 __42__
(Hour of reporting)

This Local Board will furnish transportation to an induction station of the service for which you have been selected. You will there be examined and if accepted for training and service, you will then be inducted into the stated branch of the service.

Persons reporting to the induction station in some instances may be rejected for physical or other reasons. It is well to keep this in mind in arranging your affairs, to prevent any undue hardship if you are rejected at the induction station. If you are employed, you should advise your employer of this notice and of the possibility that you may not be accepted at the induction station. Your employer can then be prepared to replace you if you are accepted, or to continue your employment if you are rejected.

If you are not accepted, you will be furnished transportation to the place where you were living when ordered to report for induction by this Local Board.

Willful failure to report promptly to this Local Board at the hour and on the day named in this notice is a violation of the Selective Training and Service Act of 1940 and subjects the violator to fine and imprisonment. Bring with you sufficient clothing for 3 days.

You must keep this form and bring it with you when you report to the Local Board.

If you are so far removed from your own Local Board that reporting in compliance with this Order will be a serious hardship and you desire to report to a Local Board in the area of which you are now located, go immediately to that Local Board and make written request for transfer of your delivery for induction, taking this Order with you.

_____
Member of Local Board.

D. S. S. Form 150
(Revised 1/2/41)

NOTICE OF CLASSIFICATION

NOTE: Appeal from a classification by a Local Board or Board of Appeal must be made within five days from the date of this notice at the office of the Local Board.

The person named herein whose Order No. is 3647

Has been classified by { Local Board #255 [✓] / Board of Appeals [ ] }

in Class 1-A until ✓

(Date)

M. [signature]
Member of Local Board

May 7 - 1942
(Date)

Notify your employer of this classification

This card may be cut on dotted line for convenience in carrying.

D. S. S. Form 57

REGISTRANT—SIGN HERE: *Werner Kloman*

BE ALERT

Keep in touch with your Local Board

Notify it of any change of address

Notify it of any fact which might change your classification

Failure to notify the Board of these facts within five days of the happening thereof is an Act punishable by fine and imprisonment.

---

along with other new draftees, was taken to Governor's Island for induction and swearing in. Then we were sent to Penn Station, where we boarded a train to Camp Upton, Long Island. That was where we changed from our civilian status to military status.

After receiving uniforms, the civilian clothes were packed and sent home for the duration of the war. From then on, we were not allowed ever to wear civilian clothing.

Next came a medical exam, and after a few days' stay, we were shipped via special troop train to Camp Wheeler, in Macon, Georgia, for the 90-day basic training. Also known as "boot camp," this is

an episode of army life that is rigorous because of its utter relentlessness and grinding repetition. I have a blurry recollection of having to rise 5:30AM, doing calisthenics, marching, running, climbing, more marching, taking orders, and simply getting whipped into shape for real army life. There were three meals a day of army food, which was substantial but wholly uninteresting. Still, with stories about people literally dying from starvation in Europe, this food was just fine.

After one straight month of basic training, we got a little time off. I went with some of the fellows to a weekend party in Macon, and that was where I met a quirky but remarkable character, Freddie Strauss.

Freddie, who was the sergeant, and was Jewish, came over to me and said, "Soldier, where do you come from?" I said, "New York," and he replied, "and your accent....you must come from Germany." I said "Yes," and we started to talk. Our conversation led us to recognize that Freddie's mother and mine were second cousins. His mother came from a town in which my mother had family! So in a sense, we were relatives.

Freddie had already finished his basic training and worked in regimental headquarters. He took me under his wing, so to speak, and we became good friends. I liked Freddie but he really was something of a spoiled brat who couldn't take army life. He was an only child who had arrived late in his parents' life, and was so coddled that if he went into a card game and lost $100, he would call Mom and she would send him more money! Freddie's seemingly inexhaustible bank account came from the sales of his late father's men's stores. His mother had been left very well off, with loads of money in the Central Savings Bank back home. Of course, to us poor guys, the whole scenario seemed ridiculous - we couldn't call home to get $100.

But perhaps because he had been pampered, eventually Freddie cracked up under the pressure of military life. Later, when I was being shipped overseas, Freddie was being sent home to be a civilian. But we would meet up again, in better circumstances.

*   *   *   *   *   *   *   *

When we newcomers had finished our basic training, the next step was to become American citizens and I was ready to trade one allegiance for another. I had left behind the country of my birth and would now loyally commit myself as an American and I have been proud to be one ever since.

About 30 of us were taken by truck to Macon and presented in a federal court house to a judge who swore us in as United States citizens. Then the group, which was about 600 soldiers, was immediately packed onto a train and shipped to Camp Gordon, near Augusta.

Now we were members of the Fourth Motorized Division, U.S. Army. Henceforth, it was real army life: tough training, maneuvers, plenty of night activity and hardship. Most of the non-commissioned officers were from the south, and had joined up in order to find a home. Their families, mostly poor, could not feed or clothe them at home, and in the army they were fed, clothed, and received medical and dental care. It was obvious that their schooling had been very limited, and some had problems reading or writing. Their language was another problem, filled with profanities. Drinking was a fairly routine pastime for them, as long as they had some money. The PX did not help matters any, as it used to sell a low-alcohol beer for a few cents a cup or bottle.

Ignorance was rampant, which made it hard to be a Jew there. Some of these fellows thought Jews had horns. They also hated Yankees, and to them, anyone who did not speak with a southern drawl was a Yankee! Here, I was actually more of a Yankee than a refugee, both difficult positions to be in.

But the group was mixed, and there were some educated men in the company. Most senior officers were in the Army Reserve. One had to hold them in high esteem because educated or not, they were subject to being called any time danger sprang up around the world. They trained for two weeks every year and were proud to serve the country. Most of the junior officers were college graduates who had been sent to military schools for 90 days of training to become officers. We called them the "90-Day Wonders." This group was, in a sense, the backbone of the United States Army.

Some time during the Spring of 1943, while I was a private in Company K, 22nd Infantry, at Fort Dix, I was informed that I had to attend an interview for Officers' Candidate School at Fort Benning. I was somewhat surprised by this invitation, but evidently, the I.Q. test that I had taken upon entering the army showed a score that was high enough to attend this school.

In the office, a lieutenant colonel was in charge. I remember that he asked a minimal number of questions and then he excused me. A few days later, I was informed that I did not get the position, but was not given a reason. I knew my level of intelligence was certainly not the issue and assumed that I was considered a refugee with limited language, not equal to that of an American military officer. I must have looked good on paper, but in person I did not really qualify, at least according to the standards that they had set. I was disappointed, but gave it no further thought. Only later, when I was over in England, would the mystery surrounding this be resolved.

In September, 1943, the division moved from Fort Dix to Camp Gordon, Johnson, Florida, in the wilderness of northern Florida, bordering the Gulf of Mexico. The move was for us to start amphibious training to prepare for the invasion that was to be launched in Europe.

At the end of November, the division moved to Fort Jackson, South Carolina, for further training and preparation. Then we were sent to Camp Kilmer, New Jersey, where we arrived in January, 1944. On January 18th, we loaded again and were off to the docks at Fort Hamilton, where the ships had lined up for boarding and sailing to England.

I did not have a chance to say goodbye to my parents, who were living in Baltimore. Since we only got six hours' leave from Camp Kilmer, and it would have taken three hours just to reach Baltimore, I had to forego this journey. But I had last seen my parents the month before and we had said our goodbyes then. Now no further communication was possible, since they did not have a telephone.

With just a half-day's leave before embarking on my adventure, I went to see Freddie Strauss. I spent these last hours with him, after which he brought me to Penn Station. It was midnight when we said goodbye. What a terrible feeling I had, going into the unknown once more, and certainly with my life in danger. It is odd when I think that Freddie, of all people, was the last person I said goodbye to on American soil…..

6. A SOLDIER IN ENGLAND

In the bleakness of January, we made our 12-day transatlantic voyage, becoming part of a convoy of units that crossed the sea to build up the allied forces in Europe. The convoy consisted of old, British civilian ships filled with troops. The ship had rather limited facilities for our large group, and the ship's crew was so overworked that they only managed to feed us twice a day. This was not necessarily a hardship, since the menu consisted of dull English food! The bathing facilities were not much better....after a considerable wait in line, one could have a salt water shower.

The ocean was calm, but the trip was dark and monotonous. Feeling very caged in, we longed to reach the shore. Then finally, the Irish coast was in view and we knew it would not be long before we'd be in England.

Ironically, the boat landed at the port of Liverpool, from which I had departed when I first immigrated to the States. There we boarded a train to County Devon in southwestern England. Devon was very beautiful country, mostly farmland running along the English Channel, and it is blessed with soft, idyllic color and light.

* * * * * * * *

My stay in England would offer me many experiences that contributed to my growth as a human being, not just in character, but in my ability to understand people and myself. The first of these experiences was linked to my past....

Before I had gone overseas, I paid a visit to Norbert Lehman's parents and told them I might be able to see their son in London. When I got to England, though, nobody in the Fourth Division was granted any kind of leave. A brief stay in the hospital in Barnstable offered me the opportunity to at least make a call, since there was a public telephone. I called Norbert and told him I had greetings from his parents and brother, and that if I could get permission, I would come up to London and visit. He wished me well, saying that he hoped to see me. Although I did not get to see him, it did my heart good just to hear his voice. In March, 1944, I was sent to division headquarters for a job interview as a German interpreter for the Fourth Infantry Division, and was seen by a Colonel Keller. He was trying to assess my knowledge of German, my military experience, and of course, my character. Afterwards, he told me that out of the 12 men he had interviewed, he preferred me and said it was easy to see I was the best man for the job. I was to be transferred to headquarters in Tiverton, Devon. From then on my status would be "T-5," a specialist and interpreter. I thought this was a rather interesting turn of events, considering the rejection I had received earlier.

When I was transferred to Fourth Division Headquarters to assume my position as interpreter, I recognized that the officer in charge was the same person who had interviewed me back in the States. It was then that I realized that this officer was anti-Semitic, among the other prejudices that he had. He could not see himself sitting in an officers' club and have me, a Jew with a German accent, sitting next to him. That explained the rejection I had originally received, despite my high test score.

I was warned that with this promotion, there

might have been a problem in transferring me from the company to division headquarters. Since I was trained to be part of the first wave of the D-Day landing, the regiment had the power to stop my transfer. But that never happened, and I was able to report to headquarters as planned. I have often thought that this is the reason I am still alive and here to talk about this. If this transfer had, in fact, not gone through, I would probably have been in that first wave at Utah Beach in Normandy, in which so many were lost.

When I came back from the division the next day, I was called by the Battalion Commander, Colonel Teague, and made to sit down on his bunk in a tent and listen to him. He told me that he needed me as his personal guide and German-speaking soldier and asked me to stay with him. But I did not want to, as I was keen to get started working in my new capacity as interpreter. Nonetheless, it was a valuable experience to meet this colonel.

Teague was a young, strong man. In only 19 months, he had gone from First Lieutenant to Lieutenant Colonel because of his background, character and strength as a soldier and a leader of troops. A few years later, though, this very strong officer committed suicide, killing himself with the shot of a pistol. No one really knew why he did this, but we suspected that it had something to do with one of his six children. Having known him as a strong and steady officer, I felt that this act of suicide was incomprehensible, and the mystery was never solved.

*　　*　　*　　*　　*　　*　　*　　*

After I was transferred to Division headquarters, I felt that I became a different person. Suddenly, I was exposed to a select group of men and officers. Through the eyes of a newcomer like me, they all seemed a bit conceited, as though they believed themselves to be the "chosen" people.

Most of these men were reserve officers and were older. They often were veterans who were recalled to active duty because of their status. Some had been officers during the First World War and others had signed up for reserve duty to get extra pay. In a sense, they acted as though they were special soldiers whom God must have sent to win this war. Perhaps it helps to believe this when you have to wear a uniform and fight.

Brigadier General Theodore Roosevelt, Jr. (son of

former President Theodore Roosevelt), for example, was way over age to be on active duty, but with such a strong military family background, he demanded a post as far up front as possible. He had no fear and wanted to be among the first to face the real enemy of the world, the German soldiers. Roosevelt had fought in Africa during WWI and was charged with the task of supervising the training of the troops for the invasion. The relationship among these men was cordial and respectful.

They were more than willing to do whatever the general demanded of them. I felt that they led rather insular lives, though, and was aware of their unwritten rules. They lived in a very elegant, secluded home that had been hand picked for them. It was nicely furnished and provided them with every comfort.

In this mainly WASP contingent, Catholics and Jews were looked down upon and really not welcome. But I was used to that. Of course, feelings toward Jews are always peculiar. Some of the officers had never met any. Some men were downright hillbillies who, of course, had had no contact with Jews, so for them it was a new experience, perhaps not one that they welcomed.

But this was an admirable group of men who were later responsible for and prepared for the D-Day landing at Utah Beach in Normandy. It would come to be known that they had, in a sense, "walked" across the waters to the beach, and were credited with creating the best landing on D-Day. General Roosevelt received the Congressional Medal of Honor for his courage and success in this event. He deserved this, since he was a great example to his foot soldiers.

*　　*　　*　　*　　*　　*　　*　　*

Perhaps, though, the most significant "human" experience for me came in March, 1944, when I met and worked with Major Gatling, who had been transferred from the 12th Infantry Regiment to the Division Headquarters.

Gatling was a very fine, elegant gentleman of British descent with strong family roots. His father was a banker who worked in New York City and Gatling himself was a graduate of the Virginia Military Academy, which was on par with West Point. Subsequently, he graduated from Columbia Law School.

Gatling was calm, refined, considerate, and rather reluctant to speak about himself. By profession, he was a lawyer who was working on Wall Street for one of the more exclusive WASP firms. His boss on Wall Street was the Secretary of War under President Franklin Roosevelt. With one letter, Gatling could have had any job in Washington, but he wanted to be with soldiers, way up front. I took a liking to this man and he felt the same way about me. We had great respect for one another.

My first insight into his character came while we were stationed back in Camp Kilmer, NJ, just before our departure for England. Gatling had handled all details for the debarkation of the division. He prepared the troops for departure, and had arranged for the loading of the ship. When the rest of us had our last 8-hour pass to leave the post, Gatling stayed. He could not even take time off to go home and say goodbye to his wife and daughter, yet, he never complained. I was glad to be with such a leader as we prepared for a landing in France.

Gatling kept a war diary, which I later got hold of. This small entry reveals something about this gentleman's outlook toward life:

"About October1, 1942, when I had reported to the 12th Infantry Regiment at Fort Benning, we had the first encounter with the jeep. It is like a new toy that small boys were enjoying for the first time. That sturdy vehicle proved to be perhaps the most useful vehicle in the war. Within two years, the war machine must have had two million jeeps available."

Gatling's diary was useful later on when I wanted to review what had happened during the war. He was like an artist, keeping a close watch of all the events and recording them.

* * * * * * * *

Once over in England, we went on two amphibious maneuvers out in the English Channel and landed at Slapton Sands. This was so top secret that it was said that even Eisenhower did not hear about it. At the end of March, we got ready for a pre-invasion exercise, Beaver, (a code name), in which we would perform a "mock invasion." In preparation, all the local people, who were farmers, had to be evacuated because we were going to use live ammunition. These local inhabitants only got about one month's notice, and they would have to live elsewhere for about two to three months.

We traveled to the Channel to the evacuation area, where we practiced landing, pretending that this portion of the English coast was some area in Normandy. During the second maneuver, a German plane flew over and dropped some bombs on our area, but it was shot down. The navigator, who survived, was pulled out from the wreckage and he became Prisoner No.1 of the division.

During the interrogation, I learned that the German pilot had taken off from an airport that was just a few miles from my hometown. It was a special airport called Flugplatz Giebelstadt, and it was reserved exclusively for the use of military planes. Its central location made it ideal for planes going out on missions. (Later, in 1945, the Americans took over the airport and used it as a subdivision of the 8th Air Force, which was stationed in England. To this day, it is still under American control.) I would have liked to know more about the pilot, but the British did not allow Americans to interview German prisoners of war in England.

Our project did not go all that smoothly. During this exercise, some German E boats that were out on patrol from Cherbourg found our convoy and attacked it, sinking two boats loaded with American soldiers. About 800 of our men drowned, but this devastation was kept secret. Not even General Eisenhower was told about the incident.

In early May we repeated the exercise and landed again at Slapton Sands. This time the results reflected what the real landing experience might be in the very near future. In mid-May, we packed up again to move into a staging area. All this was done under strict orders of secrecy so that the German spies who were in England could not report these movements to their home base.

7. ON TO FRANCE

You might say that when we caught that first prisoner, we had been initiated and were now ready for the next step. On the afternoon of June 2nd, we left the staging area and our convoy was routed to a loading dock in Dartmouth. There, we backed up and were loaded onto the LST 282 with our three-quarter ton truck containing our personal belongings and the field equipment we needed to function in France. My jeep was not allowed to be part of the invasion fleet, so it was left behind with other equipment that would not be needed for the first few days or weeks. I felt blessed because I did not have to be the one to waterproof it for the crossing. Waterproofing was an exercise that could take as long as a week and it was not a one-man job. You had to encase all the wiring, the carburetors, etc., in a special compound. You had to make sure the muffler was protected, too. I was glad the job had been given to someone else!

I used to watch my friend, J.D. Salinger, the man who would later become such a well-known author. Every day, he used to waterproof his jeep so that it would function under water. He must have done a perfect job, because not only did the jeep's motor not die during the journey, but it landed safely on French soil, with Salinger able to drive it.

The next day, we lifted anchor and headed for France. We had the blessing of General Eisenhower, who had issued a dignified message from which we were to derive encouragement.

The skies were cloudy, the seas were rough and we were very crowded on the ship. Everyone from division headquarters was aboard, including the Chief of Staff and all officers and enlisted men. Time moved slowly, and there was little to do there, other than to look out into the Channel and watch for mines.

The mood of the American soldiers and officers selected for this operation was one of courage and positive thinking. We knew that we had to go in and win this battle, and there was never any doubt in our minds that we would succeed. The planning had been done in great detail and each of us knew which tasks were ours.

SUPREME HEADQUARTERS
ALLIED EXPEDITIONARY FORCE

Soldiers, Sailors and Airmen of the Allied Expeditionary Force!

You are about to embark upon the Great Crusade, toward which we have striven these many months. The eyes of the world are upon you. The hopes and prayers of liberty-loving people everywhere march with you. In company with our brave Allies and brothers-in-arms on other Fronts, you will bring about the destruction of the German war machine, the elimination of Nazi tyranny over the oppressed peoples of Europe, and security for ourselves in a free world.

Your task will not be an easy one. Your enemy is well trained, well equipped and battle-hardened. He will fight savagely.

But this is the year 1944! Much has happened since the Nazi triumphs of 1940-41. The United Nations have inflicted upon the Germans great defeats, in open battle, man-to-man. Our air offensive has seriously reduced their strength in the air and their capacity to wage war on the ground. Our Home Fronts have given us an overwhelming superiority in weapons and munitions of war, and placed at our disposal great reserves of trained fighting men. The tide has turned! The free men of the world are marching together to Victory!

I have full confidence in your courage, devotion to duty and skill in battle. We will accept nothing less than full Victory!

Good Luck! And let us all beseech the blessing of Almighty God upon this great and noble undertaking.

Dwight D Eisenhower

There were a few senior officers aboard who had served in WWI. They were our leaders, and with their presence, the atmosphere was low key. I am sure each of us had his own fear, but we felt that the Germans had an even greater fear. They had bragged about their fortress, how strong it was and how they'd push invaders back into the sea.

Despite the gloomy, gray weather and the ever-present fear that German planes might attack us, the crossing was actually uneventful. We each had our own way of calming our nerves. Mine was to read, and to focus my attention on the leaders on board whom I admired, particularly Major Gatling. He had played a meaningful role in my life as a soldier, and would continue to as time went on.

The emotional element of the journey was certainly something to consider, but the practical one really dominated our daily life. There were about 5,000 ships on the Channel at all times, and every one of them was loaded to the rafters with men, equipment and supplies for survival. We lived on K rations – mostly crackers and cheese — and C rations — beans, vegetables, cigarettes, powdered coffee. It was amazing that one actually could live on this stuff! Even the box, which was made of waxed paper, could be used as a little stove for heating the food. The navy supplied hot coffee around the clock.

I cannot say now why I was inclined to save so many documents and little pieces of paper associated with army life, but I am glad I did. I saved one of my ration cards, which is dated 2 July 1945. It is like a tiny book that is incredibly well organized. Divided into eight columns, each one representing a different week, it has many small boxes to check off. It is just as good and clear as any spreadsheet used in business today.

Studying this little card offers a good clue as to what soldiers needed the most: cigarettes, matches, soap, candy and gum. There are also blank spaces in which one could write specific items. There, in miniscule script, is my own order

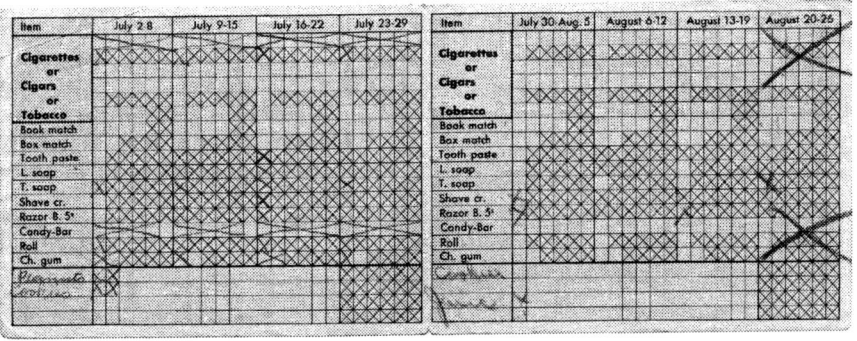

for peanuts, cookies, and juice. Seeing this card is a bit like looking through a keyhole into a secret life that is long gone.

Back on board ship again…..it seemed that the men in the navy carried everything they owned with them. They had to be fed, clothed and supplied with ammunition and fuel. We had our own items that had to be carried into France: a duffel bag that held an extra uniform, underwear, one pair of shoes, grooming articles, a blanket and half-tent. Then there was potable water for drinking and cooking as well as water for washing. The three-quarter ton truck that was aboard held a folding table and chairs which could serve as a sort of mini-conference room or an office. There were also typewriters, a full complement of office supplies, and a safe containing about $40,000 worth of French "invasion" money. This was "French" money that the American army printed in advance, in anticipation of our landing in France. We would need this later, when the division would occupy a house or chateau for our headquarters. Of course, we knew that the owner of the domicile would need to be paid for its use. (We also had German invasion money, which was quite ornate, in the

typically prewar European style. The photo shows an American made German "Mark," which was signed by Ernest Hemingway.)

There were also some "special guests" aboard the ship: our truck carried the General's pet dog, Benji, whom we would have the honor of delivering to the General, who had landed in France earlier that day. There was also a case of pigeons that were trained to fly back to England, carrying the first film of the invasion, which was tied to their legs. As it turned out, the sea crossing confused the poor birds and instead of flying to England, they flew to France and came down near Le Harvre, exhausted. We learned later that the Germans developed the film and printed the pictures in their newspapers with captions that said the Germans had sunk our boats. Clever propaganda!

D-Day was June 6, 1944. At 10:15AM, we were transferred from the ship to a raft that would carry us to the beach. Then the announcement came that the company of seabees, a special naval unit that was aboard, was also to reload onto small boats. Their mission was to go onto the beach at midnight before D-Day and destroy underwater obstacles so that the regular troops could land safely. These sailors were exposed to dangerous conditions, both on shore and in the sea. Their special equipment was lying at the railing on one side, ready to be reloaded on a small boat to take them to the beach, under cover of darkness. We eyed this with awe, knowing that an air attack could easily blow up the entire ship. This was like a suicide mission, but it had to be done. We knew that Field Marshal Irwin Rommel, who was the commanding general of the entire western front, had installed steel posts, on top of which mines were placed, and they could tear open any ship that approached. The seabees did a good job and cleared open several lanes where the landing craft could enter the area.

When we reached the beach, I was one of the first to get off and plough through the water, which was up to my shoulders. I had chosen not to use a raft. It did not feel safe and there was no way to protect oneself. A soldier had more of a chance of survival on land, where you could find some shelter. Some soldiers followed along the seawall, or dug trenches in the sand.

A couple of hours later, the small convoy reached an area that was to be the first command post and then another post was set up about four miles inland. The Infantry did an excellent job of opening the beach for us and the Fourth Infantry Division's first waves landed safely on that famous stretch of sand called Utah Beach. The smoothness of the operation was really quite miraculous. The American troops were lead by Brigadier General Theodore Roosevelt. Fearless, this man was the first American officer to wade ashore and wipe out whatever resistance he encountered.

Once we were on the beach we saw hundreds of little flags, bearing the warning, "*Achtung, Minen*!" (Attention! Mines!) but the mines turned out to be dummies. There were, in fact, no mines in the ground, which we learned as we pulled out the flags, and no explosions occurred. Rommel must have run out of mines, but not out of signs. I wondered if he had done this on purpose, since he was later involved with the plan to kill Hitler. Lucky for us that the German army had no commander there that day. Rommel was home in Herringten, with his wife, celebrating her birthday.

By the time we came ashore with our trucks, we

saw that some soldiers had already been killed and were lying in a ditch before the seawall. Artillery shells were coming from different directions, but we managed to leave the beach area safely. We drove inland for about four to five miles to find Division headquarters. Despite the casualties, we felt relieved, knowing that we were in France, the fortifications were destroyed and the war had started.

I was able to communicate with my parents during my stay in Europe, but the process was a bit cumbersome. The photo shows me sitting in a field in Normandy, writing a letter home on D-Day Plus One. The mail was called "V Mail," which meant an open letter. All letters were photographed and the film itself was sent to the U.S. This was a way of speeding up communication (which was slowed down as a result of censoring) and also saving the weight of sending paper. It took about five days for a letter to reach my parents, which is only a little more time than it takes today for a letter to get to an overseas destination.

* * * * * * * *

After a day or two in France, Major Gatling set out to visit the first towns and villages in our area. A champion walker, Gatling made his first mission a hike to St. Mère Eglise, where he met with the mayor and the officers from the Airborne Divisions occupying the town. Here is another entry from Gatling's diary that shows his ability to see the beauty and value in all of life, no matter where he was:*"D-Day, 5:30PM: The division Command Post was about one mile inland near St. Marie DuMont. It was clustered around a farm house. We got our K-rations out and went to work with*

supper. This particular farm was untouched and was as peaceful as a place 1,000 miles away from the war zone. The farmer (le paysan) seemed to be going about his business with this coterie of children as assistants. There were cows, pigs donkeys, chicken, ducks, goats, geese, cats, dogs and rabbits much in evidence. I will never forget that pastoral and peaceful scene at my first stopping place in France."

*   *   *   *   *   *   *   *

While Gatling was on his hike, I was back at headquarters since I did not speak French, and while he was gone, I started to dig a foxhole for him. When he returned, he reprimanded me for having done this! He would not accept such a service....he wanted to dig his own foxholes. This was the type of man he was.

Two nights later, we were shelled in the area by artillery and a Colonel Stone came to my foxhole to ask me if he could crawl in with me to be safe. Unlike Gatling, Stone did not want to go to the trouble of digging out a foxhole for himself. Was I going to say no to the Colonel? Of course not. He did crawl in, but a half an hour later he left again, without thanking me. Two such very different men....such a contrast of experiences.

During those first weeks in France, I took over the welfare of the section, which meant I was responsible for about eight or nine people. I drew the rations, water and other items needed for daily life, such as clean clothes and gasoline. Everything had to be brought into France — even toilet paper! Laundry was a problem because there were no facilities available. We had to wash our clothes and ourselves in the refreshing, cold water of a woodland stream.

In the middle of June, 1944, all the jeeps belonging to the G-5 Section, Fourth Division were brought into Normandy. Finally, we had our own transportation! I immediately took possession of my jeep, with the generic license plate number HQ 73. Gatling's jeep had a more personal plate: "Blue Ridge." He had named it after the region where he had his roots. This kind of sentimentality was part of Gatling's charm.

* * * * * * * *

Our next mission was to turn right and fight our way into Cherbourg, about 25 miles north. I drove into Cherbourg to see what the general conditions were. The first question I asked civilians in my limited French was, *"Les juifs sont ici?"* (Are there any Jews here?) and their answer was always the same: "*Les juifs sont partis*," (The Jews are gone). So now we knew there were no Jews left in Cherbourg. This would be the first of many reports that would be almost too much to grasp. It gave me an inkling into what had already transpired before our arrival. I would later have to pass this news along to the division rabbi, who would be equally shocked.

When the Jewish Chaplain, Rabbi Morris Frank, arrived, he had made a visit was to a military cemetery that had been established near St. Mère Eglise. To the rabbi's puzzlement, there did not appear to be any Jewish graves. He studied the situation and found the Jewish boys were buried with crosses on their graves. The rabbi went to the man in charge of the cemetery and inquired. He was told that the boat carrying the Stars of David had sunk in the Channel! He asked, then, that the crosses simply be removed, out of respect.

* * * * * * * *

After a time I realized that without the ability to speak French, it was going to be hard for me to gather much intelligence from the local people. I decided on another route: I checked myself into the Cherbourg's German Naval Hospital as a military supervisor and observer. I thought that the Gestapo and some high ranking SS officers might check in, posing as wounded men in the hope that no one would realize they were Nazi war criminals. They knew that as POW's, they'd be treated better. After several hours of careful listening and watching in the hospital, though, I could not find any evidence of this kind of ruse. Additionally, the odor of the hospital's poisonous chemicals was intolerable. I knew I had to get out, so I drove my jeep to the Hotel Atlantique, where the Division headquarters had been established.

At the hotel, I set up a place to sleep under a table in the hotel lobby. Because of explosions outside and around the hotel, plaster fell from the walls all night long. In the morning I was quite grumpy and before leaving, I helped myself to one of the hotel's beautiful woolen blankets, embroidered with the hotel's name. Somehow, I never used the blanket, since I already had two Army blankets, but it would come in handy at a later date.

Several months later, on a November night, while we were stationed in Zweifall, Germany, J.D. Salinger, who was fighting alongside us, suddenly received an order from his drunken commanding captain. It was about 9PM and Salinger was told to go and stay in the foxhole with his regiment for the night. I felt sorry for him, and then remembered the blanket I had pinched from the Hotel Atlantique. I gave it to him, along with a pair of woolen socks that my mother had knitted and sent to me. He thanked me and left.

The next day when I met up him, I asked, "How was the night?" He told me that, contrary to the captain's orders, he had found a place to sleep in a house a few blocks away and did not, in fact, go to the regiment to sleep in the soggy, snow-filled foxhole!

*   *   *   *   *   *   *   *

Once Cherbourg was in American hands, the war picture changed. On the peninsula where Cherbourg lay, we moved south toward the beaches where we had first landed. The weather was foul. It rained relentlessly for several weeks, grounding all planes that were needed to open new sites for us in central France. Then suddenly, on July 25th, the weather cleared up and word came that the largest attack yet would be dealt to the Germans, starting at 10AM.

That morning I got an order from the Corps Commander to bury dead cattle that had been killed by artillery fire from both the Germans and the Americans. The commander did not want the soldiers to have to face these cadavers, much less inhale the dreadful odor they emitted. I had several Frenchmen to assist with this work while I drove my jeep and dragged the animals into the shell holes.

I was cleaning out some fields right up to the front lines when suddenly, I was given an order to leave. The first waves of 350 fighter bombers came over and released their loads over a very small area, about 6,000 yards long and 2,500 yards wide. The attack sounded like an earthquake. And then, just as the dust was settling, another group of 1,200 heavy bombers flew over and released their bombs in the same area. Then a third bombing occurred, and then a fourth. And so, within one hour, 3,000 planes had dropped their deadly bombs. This bombardment, which was the largest ever of a small area, sent the message to the Germans that they would not be able to continue functioning.

While I was up near the front lines during the bombardment, I must have been very close to disaster. My ears started ringing in a peculiar way and I felt the shock of the explosions as the bombs fell all around us. I crawled under a kitchen table near the wall of a barn. Soon after, I perceived someone else next to me. The two of us just froze in place and prayed, knowing our lives could end at any moment. I later learned that the man by my side was Ernie Pyle, who was a well known war correspondent who happened to be visiting the Fourth Division that day. He later admitted in some writings that he penned that he was, at that moment, scared as hell!

Ernie came to be known in various syndicated publications as "the common man's reporter." He was not interested in the life of officers, but rather, liked to report about what was happening to the everyday kind of guy. With his writing, he became enormously popular and well known.

Although this bombardment took place on July 25th, Pyle wrote his dispatch on August 9th because all dispatches went through a censor in Eisenhower's office. This was a method of preventing the enemy from getting any information. In two separate dispatches, Pyle describes his experiences during these bombardments. In one of them, he mentions lying next to an officer, and I recognized myself in this piece of writing. Of course, I was not an officer, but Pyle probably mistook me for one because I was dressed decently. We were both lucky to come out alive. Right near us was the second highest ranking military officer from Washington, General McNair, who was watching the spectacle. He was not so lucky and was killed by our own bombs. Below is part of Ernie Pyle's dispatch from that day, which is found in the book *In Normandy*, by David Nichols. It is from the chapter entitled "An Inhuman Tenseness: France: June 1944 – September 1994."

Many times I've heard bombs whistle or swish or rustle, but never before had I heard bombs rattle. I still don't know the explanation of it. But it is an awful sound.

We dived. Some got in a dugout. Others made foxholes and ditches and some got behind a garden wall – although which side would be "behind" was anybody's guess.

I was too late for the dugout. The nearest place was a wagon-shed which formed one end of the stone house. The rattle was right down upon us. I remember hitting the ground flat, all spread out like the cartoons of people flattened by steam rollers, and then squirming like an eel to get under one of the heavy wagons in the shed.

An officer whom I didn't know was wriggling beside me. We stopped at the same time, simultaneously feeling it was hopeless to move farther. The bombs were already crashing around us.

We lay with our heads slightly up – like two snakes – staring at each other. I know it was in both our minds and in our eyes, asking each other what to do. Neither of us knew. We said nothing.

We just lay sprawled, gaping at each other in a futile appeal, our faces about a foot apart, until it was over.

There is no description of the sound and fury of those bombs except to say that it was chaos, a waiting for darkness....

The results of this attack were dramatic: the Germans were in complete shambles and they suffered tremendous losses. I suffered a loss, too – one that would stay with me my whole life: the partial loss of my hearing. I was hospitalized in August of 1944 with what was called "moderately severe" defective hearing. But nothing could be done, and I was soon discharged and classified as "Full Field Duty."

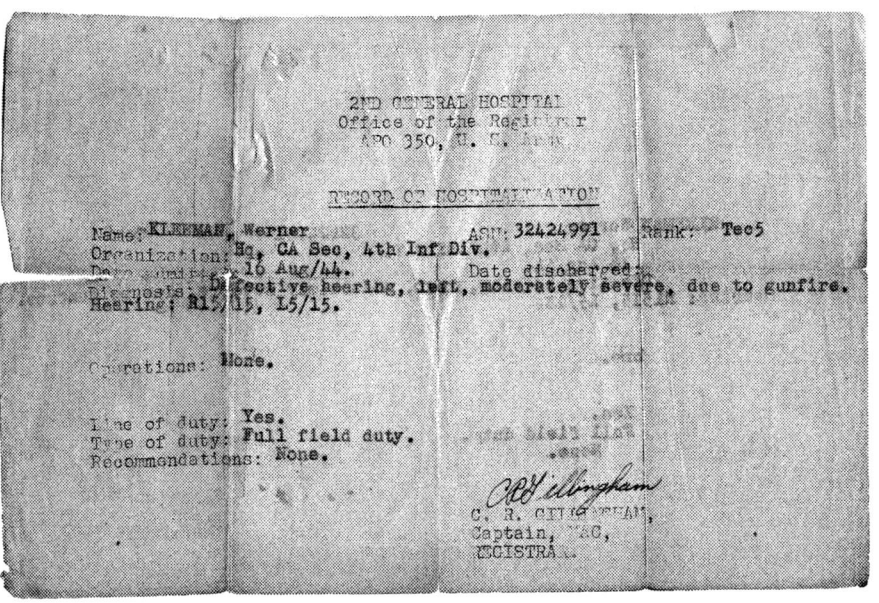

But now we had accomplished our mission: to open a portal through which General Patton could launch his Third Army and start the war the way he wanted to. It worked well and within a few days, Patton's army was rolling across central France and the Germans were on the run.

Most of the German generals realized then that the war was lost for them and Rommel was ready to make peace with the Allies. He had a peace proposal written up and carried it in his pocket. It was known at that time that Hitler did not like Rommel and suspected that he was not to be trusted....

Meanwhile, the interrogation team of the 22nd Infantry Regiment had a German soldier who claimed that he could pinpoint on a map the exact location of Rommel's headquarters. He did this and so direction was given to the Air Force for action. The Air Force bombed the road leading to the headquarters and while driving there, the German soldier's car was hit by a bomb. Rommel was badly wounded and lay unconscious for a week or more.

Rommel's days as a general were over. After a stay in the hospital, he was ordered to house arrest for having been part of a plot to kill Hitler. As he awaited further instructions, the order to execute him came in, so he was forced to commit suicide by taking a cyanide pill.

By August 24th, Paris was ready to free itself and fight the Germans who were stationed there. They asked the American army to help them, as the French armored division was not capable of freeing and re-occupying the city. The Fourth Division was chosen for this task and within 24 hours, the division was on a 120-kilometer march toward Paris.

*   *   *   *   *   *   *   *

Despite the fact that a war was going on and the world was in such serious trouble, the Fourth Infantry Division operated like a private club, a microcosm of society. There were petty rivalries, conflicts, internal political struggles and colorful characters.

First, there was General Barton, who had taught military science at Georgetown State University. One of his students was Philip Hart, a very smart fellow, and the Colonel told him that if there were ever a war, he would like to have him in his command. Hart promised he would cooperate with this request. When the war started, Hart wrote to the general about the promise he had made, and went in as a reserve officer and became Aide to General Barton.

After landing in Normandy, though, young Hart was wounded by shrapnel and was sent to England for surgery and treatment. He came back to the bivouac in November and could not use his wounded arm, but he refused to go home. It was then that a Lieutenant Bailey was sent as a replacement for Hart.

Lieutenant Bailey came from a highly respected southern family. He was the son of Senator Bailey, a Democrat from Raleigh who was a close friend of President Franklin Roosevelt. When some of the officers saw his resume, they already hated him. He had been an FBI agent, had a private pilot's license, and was the son of a senator. He was quite the outdoorsman, too. The officers were jealous of his background and never accepted him as an equal. Only Colonel Gatling showed him sincerity and respect.

The first thing Bailey did when he came in was get married by proxy. He wanted his wife to get an allotment so she could live comfortably while he was in the army. We watched the ceremony, which had to be witnessed by an officer.

The friction among the men grew to bitter controversy. A colonel and a major filed a report about Lieutenant Bailey, saying that he was not fit to be promoted to the rank of Captain. That was too much for him, and he finally transferred to the 106th Division to start a new life. This is what politics can do, even when a person is sworn in to fight and protect in the interests of the country.

Then there was Major MacPherson, a medical doctor with a rather quirky nature. I came to know him while in Normandy when I had to patrol a forward area. MacPherson came from coal mining country in West Virginia, and was used to treating miners, not soldiers. His responsibility was to treat enlisted men at his aid station, which was situated in a barn, and ship them off to the Fourth Division Aid Station for evacuation to a hospital.

Because MacPherson was a WWI veteran, in a sense he was working "overtime" by participating in WWII, and this affected his attitude. One night I came upon two American officers, First Lieutenant and Captain of a three-quarter ton truck. They said they were lost, and told me that they had both been shot through the arm and needed medical help. They did not say that it was enemy fire. To me it looked like it might have been self inflicted wounds, but I did not ask them any questions. I told them that I could lead them to headquarters, where they would find a doctor who would treat them. I brought them safely back to my headquarters and woke up MacPherson, who was asleep in the barn.

He did treat the American officers, but did it somewhat grudgingly. The next day, he called me aside and told me not to bring "strangers" to him anymore. He said he did not feel he was obligated to look after them! I felt like reporting him, but this would have been a strike against me. Officers were known to stick together and no doubt, they would have protected him and would spread the word that he had never said any of it. So I kept quiet about the incident.

8. BELGIUM AND BEYOND

After the liberation of Paris, the Fourth Infantry Division headed north toward the Belgian border. We liberated St. Quentin, Houfalize and other towns along the way. We traveled through the Ardennes and Bastogne. From there, the road led to Luxembourg and into Germany. The last cities in Belgium to be liberated were Malmedy and St.Vith, both disputed by changing hands between the Belgians and the Germans. These towns have histories similar to that of Alsace Lorraine, for they were regions whose allegiances and official languages were forced to change after every war.

From St.Vith the road led toward Bleialf and the German border. On September 12th, we crossed a little stream. On the other side was German soil, a village called Elcherath. The Germans had just pulled out and we found the warm food that they had left on a table in a farmhouse.

When I crossed the stream I encountered Colonel

Dowdy, the commanding officer of the Second Battalion, 22nd Infantry. I knew the Colonel well enough from my days in the 22nd Infantry Regiment. I quickly ran to my jeep and got a bottle of cognac for him. He thanked me and went on his way, as I went on mine. My last encounter with the Colonel will always be engraved in my memory because two days later, I heard that he had been killed while approaching the Siegfried Line, or West wall, which was the German fortification. The wall was made of concrete dragons' teeth, which were cement walls about three feet high that even tanks could not cross. The only way to get over the dragons' teeth was to bulldoze them or destroy them with explosives.

The same day, at the command post of the 22nd Infantry Regiment, I met the First Sergeant of my old Company K, Sergeant Sharpton, with whom I had a particularly warm relationship. This sergeant was a professional soldier, way above the standards of most others. Tragically, he was also killed within the next few days. The moment I learned this, a pain pierced me deeply, and it has never gone away.

*   *   *   *   *   *   *   *

Fourth Division Headquarters then moved into a wooded area near Bleialf and operated from there. The 22nd Infantry Regiment occupied the village of Buchet. Bleialf was about a mile from the West wall and this regiment had broken through the impregnable wall itself.

It was in Buchet that Ernest Hemingway joined the 22nd Regiment as a war correspondent for *The Saturday Evening Post*. He was followed by the artist John Groth, who was a correspondent for *Parade Magazine*. War correspondents wore uniforms with a special insignia, but did not carry guns. They were allowed to get as close as they wanted to the military action in order to record it, either in words or pictures. Colonel Lanham, who was in charge, was glad to have people of such high exceptional people as these two in his command. Hemingway had become a special friend of the colonel and encouraged Groth to join them.

It was interesting to observe the exchanges between these men. In Buchet we had to eat and sleep in the potato cellar of the farm house, to be safe from artillery fire, which in fact did occur. One night, the windows were rattling, plaster was falling off the walls. Hemingway stayed calm while Groth became scared and nervous. Hemingway calmed Groth, telling him, "Keep eating your meal. You'll get ulcers if you stop every time you hear a shell coming in." Two sensitive artistic men, with two distinct reactions to the same circumstances.

Groth had a pivotal, life-changing experience on September 25, 1944, when Captain Fiset, about whom I will tell more later, received orders to evacuate all civilians from Bleialf. Fiset felt that civilians were not to be trusted, since there could be spies among the population. It was a time when everyone was suspect. Trucks were to be sent the next day to evacuate the civilians, with the exception of a few men who would stay behind to take care of the livestock.

What a scene it was! The parish priest assisted us in preparing the civilians to be ready to be loaded into trucks as they came in. The trucks were parked in the middle of town and were loaded very fast, since the German army was close enough to observe this maneuver. We were on a little hill, and shells landed right on the spot where, moments before, people had been standing. Every time a truck pulled out, German artillery came right into the square where the trucks had been parked to load the civilians. It was pure luck that no one was killed.

At around 12 noon, we went into a local *gasthaus*, as inns were called — the Gasthof Zwicker, and searched for food. In the basement, we found some aged cheese and wine, which made a rather substantial lunch, quite different from what we would normally have eaten. With our hunger satisfied, we loaded another group of civilians onto the trucks and sent them away. We evacuated 220 adults, 81 children and two sick people to St.Vith.

It was on this day that Hemingway and Groth showed up to observe the evacuation. We opened the headquarters at Gasthof Zwicker, overlooking the town square, and Groth occupied the picture window, where he could observe the action and record it with pen and paper. While all of this urgent activity was taking place, we saw him sitting in the bay window, drawing pictures. He did not speak to anybody. He just kept to himself and drew, and then went away again with Hemingway. We noted that he had asked Captain Fiset for his name and where he came from.

In the middle of November, Captain Fiset received a letter from his father, who was living in Chicago. With this letter came two pages from

Parade Magazine, which was enclosed in leading newspapers throughout the United States. These pages contained all the drawings that Groth had made of the evacuation of the civilians that day. Of course, Capt. Fiset's father was proud of his son for having done such a fine job.

*   *   *   *   *   *   *   *

After some time, the movement of the Division

then became stagnant and was in the vicinity of Bullingen, Belgium. We stayed there for about a month and just watched the enemy lines. Then we relocated to the Hürtgen Forest area and settled down in Zweifall for three weeks. There was very little movement through the forest.

While in Zweifall, I had a special assignment. Every morning, I was to drive out about five kilometers to a farm that resembled a Texas ranch. It had a modern house, a barn for cows, and many acres under cultivation. My task was to pick up milk for the town's children.

One morning, the mistress of the house, Frau von Lindenau, asked me if she could see an officer. I agreed to this and the next morning I asked Major Fiset to accompany me and meet with this woman. She had just one question for him: "Do you know a Major Collins?" As it turned out, the person she was referring to was General Collins, the Corps Commander. Frau von Lindenau admitted to us that years ago, while Collins was on occupation duty during the First World War, she had kept company with him. His command post was just a few miles away. I can only imagine that he must have been shocked when he got this news of an old flame looking for him.

*   *   *   *   *   *   *   *

On December 5th we moved to Luxembourg for a rest period. The infantry had to patrol the front line along the Saur River that separates Luxembourg from Germany. All was quiet until December 16th, when the Germans launched their last offensive battle.

The attack came during the night. It was so severe that two of the regiments of the 106th Division were captured before they had a chance to realize what was happening. That was the largest single defeat for the army during WWII. The Fourth Division was hit hard at the Luxembourg border, but it succeeded in stopping the Germans in their advance. They never broke through our lines and might have gained a few miles in territory, but they were stopped from advancing further into Luxembourg. After that, we slowly regrouped and moved forward again to regain the area that the Germans had taken from us. This was done by the end of February and we moved through the Schnee Eifel where we had first settled in September of 1944.

When it was clear that Germany was losing the war, the American army distributed pamphlets, which they had printed by the thousands, among the German soldiers. The pamphlets were written by an American psychologist, who felt this was the best way to tell German soldiers to surrender. We never did learn the extent of the effectiveness (if there was any) of these documents.

WHAT IS THE VALUE OF YOUR LIFE?

For your mother who brought you into this world under pain and sacrificed for you her own bread, to let you grow up—Everything

For your wife who loves you with all her heart and is waiting at home for you and hopes you will return.—Everything

Your child who needs you to help him grow up and looks to you to lead him through life in the world. —Everything

For your homeland that needs you to help rebuild it for a new future after the war—Everything

For your leaders, who know that the war is lost and demand that you serve under impossible conditions against a superior power. —Nothing

Was ist ein Leben wert?

Für Deine Mutter, die Dich unter Schmerzen in die Welt setzte, die sich vielleicht das Brot vom Munde absparte, um Dich grosszuziehen —

ALLES

Für Deine Frau, die mit ihrem ganzen Herzen an Dir hängt, die auf Dich wartet, die bangt und hofft, dass Du zurückkommst —

ALLES

Für Dein Kind, das Dich als Erzieher und Ernährer braucht, das zu Dir als seinem Führer auf dem Weg in die Welt aufschaut —

ALLES

Für Deine Heimat, die Dich zum Wiederaufbau und für eine neue Zukunft nach dem Kriege braucht —

ALLES

Für Deine Führung, die weiss, dass dieser Krieg verloren ist, und Dich trotzdem gegen eine überlegene Macht immer wieder rücksichtslos einsetzt —

NICHTS

<u>WER SCHÄTZT DEN WERT DEINES LEBENS RICHTIG EIN?</u>

Wenn Du Deiner Frau, Deiner Mutter, Deinem Kinde glaubst, wenn Du Deine Heimat liebst, gibt es nur einen Ausweg:

SCHLUSS MACHEN!

Who tells you the real value of your life?

If you hope to see your wife, your mother or children, if you want to see your city or village again, there is only one way.

BRING THIS TO A CLOSE

You will be removed immediately from the battle zone.

You receive the same food and rations as the allied soldiers.

You have a right to mail three letters and four postcards every month and may receive letters and packages.

You receive the same pay that you received in your own unit. Voluntary work will be paid extra.

You have the opportunity to learn a profession and to study.

After the end of the hostilities, you will be sent back to your hometown at the first opportunity.

Soldiers of the 709th, 243rd and 77th Infantry Division! Soldiers of the Marine Units in Cherbourg!

Cherbourg is surrounded. No one can get out anymore. Nobody can help you escape. Seaways, land paths and airways are blocked.

Your situation is hopeless. Your commanders have written you off. You cannot salvage the situation but whoever wants to can save his own life.

dropped on Cherbourg 2 days before it was taken

SOLDATEN DER 709., 243., UND 77. I.D.!

SOLDATEN DER MARINEEINHEITEN IN CHERBOURG!

Cherbourg ist eingeschlossen. Keiner von Euch kann mehr heraus—und niemand kann Euch entsetzen. See—, Land—und Luftweg sind gesperrt.

Eure Lage ist aussichtslos. Eure Führung hat Euch abgeschrieben. Ihr könnt die Lage nicht retten—aber wer will, kann sein Leben retten.

Wer sich alliierten Truppen ergibt, kann sich darauf verlassen, dass er anständig behandelt wird. Mehr als 15,000 von euren Kameraden von den anderen Einheiten in der Normandie haben die Erfahrung schon gemacht.

Kommt einzeln oder in kleinen Gruppen. Unsere Soldaten haben Befehl, auf niemanden zu schiessen, der sich ergeben will und etwas Weisses schwenkt oder den Helm oder das Gewehr.

Wenn Ihr nicht direkt zu uns 'rüberkommen könnt, verkrümelt Euch im Gelände und wartet bis wir kommen. Am besten wartet Ihr, bis unsere Infanterie da ist. Bringt euer Kochgeschirr mit.

91/DZ

Anyone who surrenders to the allied forces can be assured that he will be treated respectfully and decently. More than 15,000 of your comrades in Normandy have done so already.

Come forward in single file or in small groups. Our soldiers have been ordered not to shoot at anyone who wishes to surrender and waves something white or his helmet or gun.

If you cannot surrender directly to us, hide in the bushes and wait until we arrive. It is best to wait until our infantry is nearby. Bring your mess dish with you.

SAFE CONDUCT

The German soldier who caries this Safe Conduct document is using it as a sign of his genuine wish to give himself up. He is to be disarmed, to be well looked after, to receive food and medical attention as required, and is to be removed from the danger zone as soon as possible.

PASSAGE DOCUMENT

To the British and American Outposts:

The German soldier who carried this passage document is using it as a sign of his own voluntary surrender. He is to be disarmed. He must be treated well. He has a right to food and if needed, medical treatment. He is to be evacuated from the danger zone as soon as possible.

A SOLDIER'S DUTY

For five years, the German soldier has done his duty on all fronts. In doing so, he has sacrificed and had many hard experiences.

SAFE CONDUCT

The German soldier who carries this safe-conduct is using it as a sign of his genuine wish to give himself up. He is to be disarmed, to be well looked after, to receive food and medical attention as required, and is to be removed from the danger zone as soon as possible.

PASSIERSCHEIN

An die britischen und amerikanischen Vorposten: Der deutsche Soldat, der diesen Passierschein vorzeigt, benutzt ihn als Zeichen seines ehrlichen Willens, sich zu ergeben. Er ist zu entwaffnen. Er muss gut behandelt werden. Er hat Anspruch auf Verpflegung und, wenn nötig, ärztliche Behandlung. Er wird so bald wie möglich aus der Gefahrenzone entfernt.

The many victories during the past five years have not helped him.

Today the Russians on the Eastern front are quickly moving forward. Rome has been liberated and the new battle in France has begun.

On all fronts the overwhelming power of the opponent armies is showing its strength. Germany has no further hope of winning this war. The Germans can only delay this action.

Your duty as a soldier has been completed.

Now you have the duty of maintaining your own safety or life.

Your family, your nation and your fatherland need healthy men for reconstruction, not men who are sacrificed to a lost generation.

As soldiers, you are guaranteed decent treatment if taken as prisoners, according to the laws of the Peace Accord of the Geneva Convention, guaranteed by the Allies.

Just reading these tells so much about the American mentality and our values during the war.

The Germans had their own pamphlets and fliers also. Seen from today's perspective, this one is particularly chilling: "What Should You do When the Enemy Breaks In?" The "enemy" is well defined in the first line of text: Americans,

Was ist zu tun wenn der Feind einbricht?

Betrachtet die Amerikaner, Engländer, Goullisten, Juden und was alles sich in ihrem Gefolge über die Grenze hereinwälzen wird, als das, was sie sind: **als Feind!**

Seht auf die Ruinen Eurer Städte und Dörfer und seht auf die Invasoren, dann seht auf die Verbrecher am Tatort! Wenn dieser Feind Euch nach dem Weg fragt, so zeigt ihm den Weg nach den Friedhöfen, auf denen Tausende Männer, Frauen und Kinder begraben liegen, die dieser selbe Feind hingemordet hat.

Könnt Ihr sie achten, die durch ihre Bomben Eure Städte, Euer ganzes Hab und Gut vernichtet, viele Kirchen und Kulturstätten geschändet, die Euch im Tiefflug auf der Straße, auf der Bahn, bei friedlicher Arbeit und Eure Kinder beim Spiel beschossen haben?

Wenn einer erwidert, daß der einzelne Franzose oder Amerikaner unschuldig sei, so denkt daran, wieviel **unschuldiger** die friedlich arbeitenden Volksgenossen, vor allem die Frauen und Kinder waren, die er unter Bombenteppichen und in Feuersbrünsten grauenvoll umgebracht hat?

Laßt Euch nicht provozieren, wahrt äußerste Zurückhaltung! Frauen und Mädchen werft Euch nicht weg. ...tt an Eure Männer, Söhne und Brüd... ... feldgrauen Rock.

...der von den fremden ... ...sie werden den Kleinen vielleicht zuerst Schokolade ... ... zu nehmen.

...usam... ...rbeitet, wer seiner Kriegsmacht freiwill... ...leistet, wer seinen Soldaten ...te der Höflichkeit macht, übt Verrat an seinem deutschen Volk und wird die Folgen zu ... Mit Verrätern wurde zu allen Zeiten kurzer Prozeß gemacht und der Arm der Gerechtigkeit ...weit!

Werdet Ihr mit Gewalt gezwungen, ihnen Dienste zu leisten, so merkt Euch die Namen der Formationen, der Offiziere, ihrer Organe, gegebenenfalls ihrer zivilen Helfershelfer. Sie werden ihrer gerechten Strafe nicht entgehen. Sollten sich Volksgenossen finden, unwürdig ihres Blutes, die mit dem Feind zusammenarbeiten, merkt auch ihre Namen, sie werden in kurzer Frist zur Rechenschaft gezogen werden.

Helft allen deutschen Kameraden, die vom Feind verfolgt werden!

Es ist gewiß eine harte und schwere Bewährungsprobe, die das Schicksal jetzt von Euch fordert. Dafür wird es die letzte sein!

Denkt immer daran

...die deutsche **Wehrmacht** kämpft unbeugsam und unüberwindlich, der deutsche Arbeiter ...hafft Tag und Nacht für den technischen Ausgleich, Großdeutschland umfaßt ein ...lk von 85 Millionen, entschlossen, seine Freiheit, seinen Lebensraum und seine **Zukunft** ...ehaupten, Europa vor dem Zugriff des Bolschewismus und des Judentums zu retten.

Der Führer ist der Garant des kommenden Sieges.

Vergeßt nicht: Wir werden niemals kapitulieren!

Wir kommen wieder!   Es lebe der Führer!

English, French, Jews, and all those who cross the border unlawfully. One would think, in reading this document, that the Germans had done nothing to wage war on all of Europe! They bemoan the loss of their countrymen as well as their churches and cultural landmarks. One wonders if the local "Volk" really thought that their government was innocent and had done nothing to provoke the attack.

10. BACK TO GERMANY

By September, my unit was across the border into Germany. My job was to go in and set up the occupation governments in these districts, each of which had its own military team. Our goal was to "clean house," that is, select people whom we could question, and have the Nazis arrested.

Now the American government would be the powerhouse in Germany. The occupied area was ours. The first thing we did was post large proclamations on the key buildings of the town square. There, in black and white, the proclamations stated that the Americans had come "as conquerors, but not as oppressors."

Some of the language in these majestic documents still sends chills through my body. It shows such single-mindedness and imparts a victorious and democratic tone:

MILITARY GOVERNMENT—GERMANY
SUPREME COMMANDER'S AREA OF CONTROL

PROCLAMATION No. 1

TO THE PEOPLE OF GERMANY:

I, General Dwight D. Eisenhower, Supreme Commander, Allied Expeditionary Force, do hereby proclaim as follows:—

The Allied Forces serving under my command have now entered Germany. We come as conquerors, but not as oppressors. In the area of Germany occupied by the forces under my command, we shall obliterate Nazi-ism and German Militarism. We shall overthrow the Nazi rule, dissolve the Nazi Party and abolish the cruel, oppressive and discriminatory laws and institutions which the Party has created. We shall eradicate that German Militarism which has so often disrupted the peace of the world. Military and Party leaders, the Gestapo and others suspected of crimes and atrocities will be tried and, if guilty, punished as they deserve.

II.

Supreme legislative, judicial and executive authority and powers within the occupied territory are vested in me as Supreme Commander of the Allied Forces and as Military Governor, and the Military Government is established to exercise these powers under my direction. All persons in the occupied territory will obey immediately and without question all the enactments and orders of the Military Government. Military Government Courts will be established for the punishment of offenders. Resistance to the Allied Forces will be ruthlessly stamped out. Other serious offences will be dealt with severely.

III.

All German courts and educational institutions within the occupied territory are suspended. The Volksgerichtshof, the Sondergerichte, the SS Police Courts and other special courts are deprived of authority throughout the occupied territory. Re-opening of the criminal and civil courts and educational institutions will be authorized when conditions permit.

IV.

All officials are charged with the duty of remaining at their posts until further orders, and obeying and enforcing all orders or directions of Military Government or the Allied Authorities addressed to the German Government or the German people. This applies also to officials, employees and workers of all public undertakings and utilities and to all other persons engaged in essential work.

DWIGHT D. EISENHOWER,
General,
Supreme Commander,
Allied Expeditionary Force.

TO THE PEOPLE OF GERMANY:

General Dwight D. Eisenhower, Supreme Commander, Allied Expeditionary Force, does hereby proclaim as follows: —

The Allied Forces serving under my command have now entered Germany. We come as conquerors, but not as oppressors....we shall obliterate Nazism and German Militarism. We shall overthrow the Nazi rule, dissolve the Nazi party and abolish the cruel, oppressive and discriminatory laws and institutions which the Party has created. We shall eradicate that German Militarism which has so often disrupted the peace of the world. Military and Party leaders, the Gestapo and others suspected of crimes and atrocities will be tried and, if guilty, punished as they deserve....."

True to the President's word, we immediately implemented these and other goals. Upon entering a village, we would remove the Nazi Bürgermeister and choose someone who was not part of the system, and we would appoint *him* as the new Bürgermeister.

The photo shows me as an eager young soldier who has just been assigned to the headquarters of the 6th Army Group, which was stationed in Heidelberg. There was much work to do, what seemed like a lifetime of damage to repair, a whole society to put back together. There were broken families, ruined businesses, unjust distribution of wealth and possessions. There was pain and injury that we would not be able to repair, but there was also much that we could and *did* do.

This group picture shows the military government team on Ochensenfurt. I am at the far left of the bottom row. When I look at this photo, I remember that there was one officer whom I genuinely liked and respected – Captain Winphall. He came from the Los Angeles area.

(Many years later, in the 1970s I found myself out in that part of the country because one of my daughters was living there. I looked up the captain many times, but never could locate him. Finally, I had to give up. In everyone's life, there are always going to be some loose ends.)

*   *   *   *   *   *   *   *

As part of my personal responsibility, I made it a priority to go back to my hometown. I wanted to see it again and find a way to work there so that I could reconnect with my past and complete unfinished business.

My desire became clearer when I met up with Colonel Gatling one day. It was in the resort town of Bad Nauheim, near Frankfurt, where there was a replacement office for new military assignments. Gatling asked me up to his room for a chat. Handing me a bottle of cognac, he asked if I'd be interested in going with him to Linz, Austria, where he was to become military Governor. I told him that while I'd have liked to help him, my heart was set on going back to Gaukönigshofen. But I did agree to stay for awhile and help him out, since I knew the area and the people there. He accepted this offer with the understanding that I had other plans.

My going back to Gaukönigshofen was not really permitted by the army. It was known that I had an emotional connection, and returning to what had once been home terrain was thought to be imprudent. But I could not let that stand in my way. I was determined to find a way to get back there, work there, and complete my "mission."

```
        ALLIED EXPEDITIONARY FORCE
            MILITARY GOVERNMENT
                  OFFICE
    The bearer, T/5 WERNER KLEEMAN 32424991    ,
  a member of Mil. Gov't. Det. I-346, Ochsenfurt,
  Mainfranken, Germany, is authorized, in the per-
  formance of official duties, to enter any towns
  or villages, to contact and converse with civil-
  ians, to transport civilians in US Army vehicles
  and other vehicles. He may be required to prove
  his identity. On official duties he may be out
  after curfew hours.
                          Signature ........................
                          Date ........................
                          Detachment No. ........................
```

The first step was to join the military team in Ochsenfurt. I packed my bundle and looked for the jeep that delivered mail and papers once a day to the units and asked if I could come along. They let me come aboard and took me with them, no questions asked.

I arrived a few hours later at the military detachment in Ochsenfurt. Officially, you could say I was "absent" from my replacement depot, but curiously, no one made any effort to track me down. I had thought perhaps they'd look for me, maybe even arrest me, but that never happened, and so my plan was unhampered. I checked in at the Ochsenfurt base and began working with the people there.

An old black and white photo shows what a military office looked like at the time. Note that the woman, who is a German office worker, is wearing the traditional dirndl dress and has her hair in a bun. She has a singularly prewar look about her.

This type of quaintness was soon to disappear from German life. It was emblematic of a nationalistic spirit that would die with the end of the war, only to be resurrected in a totally different form years later, when Germany came back to life again.

*   *   *   *   *   *   *   *

*   *   *   *   *   *   *   *

A casual photo of me shows my utter delight in being in my own jeep, ready for my next adventure.

Before getting too deeply into the work routine, though, I took advantage of a well-deserved two-week furlough. I went to England, where there were several people I wanted to see. Among them was Norbert Lehman. He was happy to visit with me again, and thought he would do a good thing by arranging to take me with him for the weekend to Brighton, at the seaside, where he had a summer home.

Certainly, Norbert meant this to be a pleasant experience, but it was actually a great punishment for me. Suddenly, I was sitting once again on the other side of the English Channel, looking at water that I had never wanted to see again. The crossing in 1944 had been so treacherous and the memory of it had left me with bitter feelings. But I kept quiet and told Norbert that I was very happy to be with him.

I always knew that I was going to keep my connection with Norbert. He had played the most important role in saving my life, and I could not imagine ever losing touch with him. I will fast-forward now to say that my intention was fulfilled, and to this day, I am in touch with Norbert's granddaughter, Deborah.

Not long ago, Deborah got married, and although I could not attend the wedding, I sent a gift. Here is the text of the lovely hand-written reply she sent, which, I might add, was penned in *gold* ink!

Dearest Werner,

Thank you so very much for your best wishes and your generous gift. I knew that my father was thrilled to see the note that you sent my Aunty Joan, I can truly say that the memories you evoked helped in making the whole wedding a wonderful and very special occasion. My father felt that, in some way, his father was represented by your good wishes. I am sure he will write to you himself to try and explain (without sounding too dramatic, perhaps I can say that we felt *an echo of my grandfather's presence through your memories.)*

As for the wedding day itself, it was a truly perfect day from start to finish: lovely weather, a beautiful chuppa and very joyous celebrating afterwards. We have many happy moments to cherish for the years to come.

I do hope that we will get a chance to meet some day. (My father has a photo somewhere of the G.I. who visited him as a boy!) In the meantime, we would all like to wish you a very happy and healthy New Year.

With love and best wishes,

Deborah and Ivan

How nice to see that two generations later, the value of the relationship is still so apparent. I am grateful that this young woman is aware of the friendship I had with her grandfather – this is what makes relationships endure.

*　*　*　*　*　*　*　*

Back to the war days: on my trip to England, I also visited the uncle of a good friend of mine, Fritz Rau. Fritz's family and mine had had a business relationship before the war. They had owned a large grain warehouse in Ochsenfurt and used to buy the local "Gerste" from us, a kind of rye that was treated with water and used for brewing beer.

The history of the Rau firm is an interesting one. Before the war, it had been the largest industrial plant in the town and the largest taxpayer in the county. The facility was a block long and had access to both rail and water. The boats would come along and be loaded with the finished product to go down the local river, and from there they'd go down the Rhine. The final destination was usually Dortmund, whose beer was world famous. But with the rise of the Third Reich, the Raus lost everything. The Nazis took over the factory and installed a supply depot in the plant building for their military purposes.

The manager of the plant was a man from my village. I remember how every day, he used to pedal the six kilometers to the town to open and close the facility. It was he who had telephoned the Jews of Gaukönigshofen during the afternoon of November 10th and had told them that the Nazis would come during the night to destroy all the Jewish property.

Fritz's father was one of three brothers who

owned the warehouse. One brother immigrated to England, and he was the gentleman I visited. He told me that Fritz was still alive, having been spared because his wife was a Christian. He was living in Nürnburg, and I resolved to see him when I was back in Germany. In anticipation of that visit, I purchased a few hard-to-get gift items, like coffee. I later received a beautiful handwritten letter from Fritz, thanking me for the gifts. The letter paper itself, which is fine, European company stationery, is so evocative of the life in Europe that we used to enjoy. And Fritz's writing, executed with a fountain pen in the incredibly meticulous penmanship of prewar Europe, speaks of a way of life that will never come back. It is amazing to think that from such a dignified society arose such evil and barbarism. Still, looking at a letter such as this one, I can feel some of what was good in days gone by.

* * * * * * * *

Back in Germany again, what I found was a very mixed group of officers and men who had settled into an easy routine. Of course, I may have been considered a bit naïve, but I'd say that the lifestyle they'd set up for themselves wasn't exactly one of

MALZFABRIK OCHSENFURT
S. EM. RAU
OCHSENFURT AM MAIN
(Beste Braugerstengegend Bayerns)

**HELLSTE HOCHAUSGEDARRTE PILSNER UND DORTMUNDER SOWIE
VOLLAROMATISCHE MÜNCHNER MALZE AUS FEINSTEN UNTERFRÄNKISCHEN GERSTEN**

Telefon: In Nürnberg Nr. 24276, in Ochsenfurt a. M. Nr. 202 · Girokonto bei der Reichsbank in Nürnberg und Ochsenfurt · Postscheckkonto Nürnberg 600
Telegramm-Adressen: für Nürnberg: Malzrau, für Ochsenfurt: Malzfabrik · Eigener Bahnanschluß · Wasserversand
Geschäftsgründung 1864 · Hauptbüro: Nürnberg, Königstorgraben 1

Alle schriftlichen Mitteilungen erbitte an die
Firma S. em. Rau, Nürnberg 2, Schließfach

Ochsenfurt, den 1. November 1945.
Dr. Martin Lutherstraße 481½.

Fritz Erich Rau.

Betrifft:

Lieber Herr Kleemann!

Als ich am 11. September wieder hierher kam, fand ich zu meiner großen Freude die reiche Korrespondenz von meinen verschiedenen Verwandten und das kleine Päckchen vor, die Sie so freundlicher Weise aus Ihrem Urlaub mitgebracht hatten; erfuhr aber leider von Ihrer Erkrankung und auch davon, daß Sie betrüblicherweise nicht mehr auf Ihren hiesigen Posten zurückkehren würden. Hatte ich doch inzwischen das Ihnen Versprochene aus der Oberpfalz geholt und hätte es Ihnen so gerne ausgehändigt. So freue ich mich, gestern erfahren zu haben, daß Sie doch noch in Bayreuth seien und mir dieser Brief zu Ihnen gütigst besorgt werden soll. Vielleicht können Sie es ermöglichen, was, m[ein]e oooo, Ihr Frau und ich ganz besonders begrüßen würden, vor Ihrer wohlverdienten Heimkehr zu all Ihren lb. Angehörigen in die Brückhütt, noch einmal hier bei uns persönlich vorbeizukommen ./.

bitte wenden!

military discipline. These fellows had appropriated a private home for their own use and had hired a woman to do the cooking. She prepared three meals a day for them from the rations that came in from the depot in Frankfurt.

After lunch, they always rested for two hours, European style, and in the evenings, they engaged in "private entertainment" with Dutch girls, since fraternization with German girls was forbidden.

Within a week there, after I had settled in to my own work routine, the captain asked me to go the hospital and get some quinine tablets. I made the trip and got the quinine, but the nun in charge had to explain to me how it should be used to be effective. Little did I knw that it was being used to abort pregnancies!

The next request I received was to get my hands on a car, since each officer was supposed to have a German car for personal use on weekends. I poked around and found a fairly new Mercedes that was hidden in a barn and covered with straw. Apparently, the car's original owner had put it there for safekeeping. The roof of the car had caved in from the weight of the straw, but I was

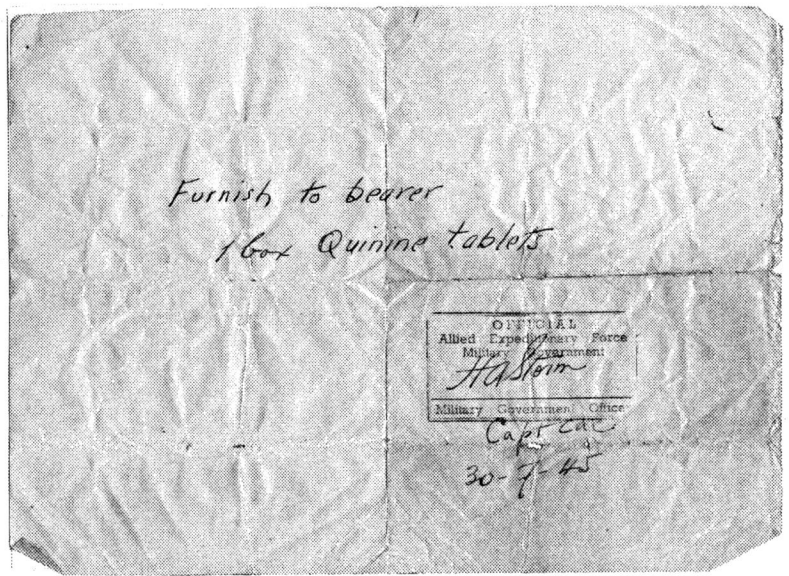

able to have it fixed by a mechanic I knew from prewar days.

When the car was ready, the first trip organized was to Garmisch, Hitler's headquarters. This destination did not interest me, because I had other plans. I took my jeep and set out first to Nürnburg, to see Fritz.

When Fritz and I visited, we sat and talked, although there was not that much to say. Mostly it was just good to be with someone from the "old days," because we had known a lot of the same people. He was grateful that I had visited his uncle on my short visit to England. We both knew that with the world so ripped apart from the war, it was a comfort to talk about and be around familiar people.

My next destination, though, was more pressing. I went to Gaukönigshofen, where I would make an "unofficial" visit, alone. To prepare the villagers for my visit, I had sent an emissary ahead of me, an American soldier in the division who was also a rabbi, and he explained to the locals that I was on my way.

I wrote a letter to the rabbi saying that as soon as the village was liberated, he should go there and see if anyone was alive. He did go, and wrote back to me to let me know he'd spoken to the Bürgermeister. He had also inspected the synagogue and advised everyone that I was coming. (The only reason the synagogue was still standing was that it was being used as a garage for the fire department and its gear, which was the old fashioned European fire fighting equipment: hand-pulled pumps on vehicles.)

When I arrived, it was quite an emotional experience for me. Here I was, back in the place from which I had been wrenched seven years earlier. And despite the word I had sent with the rabbi, my arrival was still a shock to the people there. I was alive, well and in an American uniform! The news went around very fast that I was there and the people did not like it.

I wanted to learn all I could about what had actually taken place. First, I visited an old friend of my father's. He had never been a member of the party and I trusted that he would speak from his heart. We sat down and had a little lunch together and he told me what had gone on, what happened to the Jews when they were taken away, and so on. This would only be the introduction to my experience there. In keeping with the horror I expected, I found that all the Jews had been taken from the village and none had come back.

Then I walked through the village to my ancestral family home. When I approached the door of the house, I was in tears, remembering all that we had been through. My parents had been forced under pressure to sell our beautiful house at a ridiculously low price. The village bought it and used it as a school, but at the time of my arrival, it was occupied by 50 French POWs.

Many of the same people I had known were still in town and they all recognized me. I saw face-to-face the people who had committed acts of violence on *Kristallnacht*. Although I was filled with strong feelings and many harsh words raged through my mind, I did not talk to these people. In fact, I wanted to stay far away from them. I was determined not to give them a chance to harm me a second time.

I walked around town, listening and visiting. I went to visit one gentleman who had been a very good friend of the Jews, a righteous Christian. He was very sick at the time, so I only spent one hour with him. We discussed everything that had transpired during those terrible years, and after we spoke, he told me he had something for me. He brought out a suitcase and opened it. Inside were several preserved items of Judaica: a memorial book from the Jewish congregation, a wine cup from the synagogue and a special spice box that was used on Saturday night for services. I could not believe my eyes. I did not ask him how he came to acquire these items but could see that somehow, he had managed to save them in his house. I asked him why he had done this, but he did not explain. He just handed these treasures to me.

* * * * * * * *

I spent about three weeks gathering information and then went back to visit that righteous Christian. It was then that he told me, "You'd better get out. They might be planning something on your life." But I would not leave. I was just very careful. I put a guard on the building where I slept and did not go out at night anymore. I knew that if the villagers had wanted to do away with me, they had the means to do so. In a way, I was still threatened and I was scared, although I had my American uniform, my gun, and my jeep. But I knew I still had to be careful because some Nazis who had survived the war were still entrenched in the area, and attitudes die hard.

After a month or so, I decided it was time to make my move and accomplish my original mission. I got a list of all those who had participated in the *Kristallnacht* destruction and I had the German police arrest them. I was not allowed to arrest them myself because they had not done any damage to the American army.

It was really quite simple: I told my commander, my officer, "This guy is a Nazi collaborator," or "This fellow did that to the synagogue," "This person betrayed his neighbors," etc. Of course, I told each individual why he was being arrested.

I removed the director of the jail, since he was a Nazi, and appointed a new man. Then I had all the available men arrested and had them put in the same jail I had been in, where Jews had been held. I gave strong instructions that there were to be no visitors, no packages, no contact with the outside world. They would be treated as we had been. Additionally, I made each one sign a confession about what he had done on *Kristallnacht*.

Their families, their mothers, their wives came to plead with me to let them go home, but I ignored them. I ignored everyone who tried to call on me and beg me to let them go free. I did not feel vengeful, I felt justified. After all, they knew the crimes they had committed, and they had to pay for them. They begged me to bring them back from the POW camps, which were run by the American military police, but I didn't. I ignored that request too.

With the freedom I had working with the military government, I also checked on some of the Jewish cemeteries. There was one in Schwanfeld, where my father's parents had been buried, and it had been completely devastated. I went in to see the newly appointed Bürgermeister and told him, "Tomorrow morning, you will gather all former Nazi party members and take them to the Jewish cemetery. You will have them restore every gravestone to its proper place. I will be back in one week to check on this, to see that it has been done."

I never learned the results of my all my efforts, that is, what the captain did with those people, whether he released them or not, and I did not inquire. I just left them there, sitting in jail. The victory for me was in knowing that they could not have thought it possible that a man they had persecuted and thrown out would come back and wear the good uniform and be the boss! Certainly, they never thought this could happen.

Next I visited the Jewish cemetery in Würzburg. Because the former director of this cemetery had returned from a concentration camp and was living on the grounds there, he was able to help me locate my grandmother's grave. My grandmother had passed away during the week of *Kristallnacht*. Just as tragically, perhaps even more so, I found the graves of my late wife's grandparents, the Epsteins. They had jumped out of the window of their apartment in Ludwigstrasse, the same street in which the Gestapo had its headquarters. Albert Epstein and his wife were buried alongside one another and their graves were covered with a heavy, flat stone. (Many years later, despite my mother-in-law's multiple trips to Würzburg to learn what had happened to their lovely apartment and its elegant contents, no one was ever able to determine the answer. I am sure that nothing was left of this part of the family.)

There was some satisfaction, though, in some of my efforts. I learned that a family named Frank had returned to their village (Butthard) from one of the camps in Czechoslovakia. I went down there to help them settle back into their home, which a German couple had appropriated for themselves in the Franks' absence. Like so many Jewish families, the Franks had been forced to sell their home at a minimum price, but after the war, the deeds for these bogus sales were nullified and the properties were returned to the original owners.

I spoke to the woman who was inhabiting the

house. Of course, she had no intention of leaving, but I gave the order, and I set a time limit – she had two hours to vacate the premises. She was shocked, but two hours later she was gone and the Franks rightfully regained their property. I also instructed a First Lieutenant who had a platoon of soldiers in the village to make sure the Franks would be able to live peacefully in their own home again.

I surmised that Mr. Frank must have had some kind of decent work during his stay in the camp because he looked fairly well nourished and not totally broken, as so many returning Jews did. He was one of the lucky ones – at least his life would be worth rebuilding. He and his wife had children who had gone to the U.S. before the war, and I was able to have mail sent to them informing them of their parents' return to Butthard. Now perhaps they would have some hope of re-starting their lives with some kind of normalcy.

I did the same for several of the survivors, and also made sure they were supplied with food and some of life's basic necessities. This was one way of making a concrete, visible difference for the few who returned from the horrors of Hitler's regime.

With these small acts, I was instrumental in helping some of the victims put their lives back together.

11. GOING HOME

When the war ended, the censoring of the mail ended too. Finally, I could write and communicate freely with my parents. This was the beginning of the reëstablishment of freedom, both mental and physical.

Early in September the military tracked me down and sent orders to transfer me to Austria. I refused to go, though, because I did not want to get stuck there. I had enough points to get home and checked myself into a hospital, saying that I was suffering from arthritis in my legs (which was true). With these conditions, I was able to get discharged to go home again. Like all the others, I was anxious to return home as fast as possible and rejoin families and friends.

I did not have any real plans for my life when I left Europe after the war, but somehow, I had confidence that I would find my way and carry on. The path that my life took when I came back

to the U.S. was a long, circuitous one that I never could have predicted. I left Europe at the end of November, 1945, on a hospital ship. In December

TEC 5 WERNER KLEMAN, 32 424 991

To you who answered the call of your country and served in its Armed Forces to bring about the total defeat of the enemy, I extend the heartfelt thanks of a grateful Nation. As one of the Nation's finest, you undertook the most severe task one can be called upon to perform. Because you demonstrated the fortitude, resourcefulness and calm judgment necessary to carry out that task, we now look to you for leadership and example in further exalting our country in peace.

Harry Truman

THE WHITE HOUSE

we reached the U.S. and docked in Brooklyn. My first stop was Halloran General Hospital in Staten Island, where my arthritis would be looked at.

My condition was not so bad that I could not take advantage of the 30-day pass that the military offered me. I spent this time visiting some friends and family in New York and Baltimore. People were anxious to hear about what had gone on in Europe but I, like many soldiers who returned home, did not really feel the necessity or the inclination to speak about it. Of course, the time I spent overseas had been full of excitement, especially the thrill of success in helping to destroy the Nazi regime. The whole world knew that the Nazis were fanatics bent on conquering the entire globe, and now they had been defeated. We were glad it was over and it just seemed better to look ahead instead of back.

When I returned to the hospital, I received orders to go to Hot Springs, Arkansas for treatment. I flew down with other patients and amazingly, this little trip took three days because the army had a rule: they were only allowed to fly 200 miles a day with a planeload of patients. During the various stopovers, the patients were placed in army hospitals.

After a stopover in Kentucky and one in Tennessee, we landed in what looked like a lovely resort in Hot Springs. The army had a big medical facility there called the Army and Navy General Hospital, which was run by a rotation of doctors from the famous Mayo Clinic.

The treatment consisted of a morning bath in what were reported to be "healing waters" that came right up out of the ground. It was known then that polio patients came from all over the country and had walked out after several months of these treatments! And indeed, they cured me, too.

I was then transferred to Borden General Hospital in Oklahoma, where doctors would address the hearing loss I had incurred as a result of the war. They could do little for me, though, other than teach me a bit of lip reading, so I was discharged after only one month.

Now it was time to get on with life, to find some work and to re-enter the civilian world as a contributing member of American society. I really had no idea how I was going to earn a living, but knew that I was capable and versatile enough to find my way, as I had when I first came to the U.S. as a refugee.

As a young man in Europe, I had not had time to think about a profession; the war had come and had swept away our way of life before there was time for me to complete my education. When I think about it, I do not even know what direction I would have gone if the war had never occurred. Certainly, I was not going to go into my father's grain business. In Germany, our tradition was such that only the eldest son went into the family business.

Now, at the age of 26, I could have had the opportunity to attend college. First, however, I would have needed to graduate from high school. It all seemed too lengthy and time consuming, so I decided on another route. I chose to make my own way, and would do the best I could. Looking ahead, I pondered how I would build my life here in the States....

My old friend Freddie Strauss was up in Chicago, and I decided to pay him a visit. He was glad to see me and after we exchanged news and caught up, we got down to the business of finding work for me. Freddie had a good job with the Oppenheimer Casing Company, selling natural and synthetic sausage casings, and thought I might be interested in doing the same kind of work.

I bought myself a new suit so that I could make a good impression on prospective employers. Then Freddie and I visited some nearby cities together, such as Milwaukee and Cleveland, and I was able to see how Freddie worked. It looked like a dismal job! There was a lot of traveling, which meant rising at 4AM to visit slaughterhouses. Many of these were owned by Germans, so knowing the language was a plus. But in general, it just looked like a long, long day, so when Oppenheimer offered me a sales position, I declined.

Since I had lived in New York before the war, it seemed logical to go back East and see if I could make something of myself. One of the people I had worked for offered me a job in a sweater factory in Easton, Pennsylvania. He took me there for a day to see the place, but the prospect of moving to a small coal mining town was completely unappealing. I knew I'd have to keep looking.

Back in New York, I hooked up with some of Freddie's friends. Freddie was such an outgoing person and knew people everywhere. By the time he graduated from NYU, he had made loads of connections, and I benefited from this. Through Freddie, I met Jerry Oppenheimer (no relation to the casing company family), whose brother ran a large wholesale children's clothing business. Jerry offered me a sales territory covering Alabama, Mississippi and Tennessee.

For one month, I trained with the top salesman who covered Michigan and Ohio and then I was on my own. I bought a used car and prepared to leave for my territory. The first stop was Chatanooga, which gave me the opportunity to visit once again with the rabbi who had served in my division during the war. He took me to his family's summer home on top of Lookout Mountain and we spent an evening together. It's a good thing that I took advantage of the opportunity to visit with this very special man, because only six months later, much to everyone's shock and surprise, he passed away.

The rabbi had accepted the pulpit for a large congregation in Knoxville and commuted between that city and Chatanooga on the weekends, when he conducted Shabbat services. I learned from the family on one of my visits that the rabbi had died of a heart attack right in the Knoxville airport. So ironic, I thought, that he had gone through the whole war, but died after coming home and settling in to a comfortable position of honor in the community.

Unfortunately, the job in wholesale children's clothing did not work out for me. It was not because of any wrongdoing on my part, but because of the lack of both ethics and competence in the company. When I returned to New York after my first trip down south, I learned that Mr. Oppenheimer had not delivered any merchandise to my customers! This was even more of a problem than it appears on the surface because, as often is the case in towns of the American south, many of the merchants belonged to one extended family. And that extended family was the rabbi's. It was a shameful situation, one with which I no longer wanted to be associated. I refused to go on another trip and was cheated out of any commission I might have made, but decided to cut my losses and quit altogether. My own code of ethics had been formed when I was young and had seen the way my father did business. This code would eventually serve me well as I made my way in the world as an independent businessman. But first, I had to make a few more mistakes.

Back in New York, I hooked up with someone I knew before the war who had a ladies' underwear business. He gave me his line to sell and again, I covered the Southern territory. I succeeded in selling some of the product and did make some money, but it was not long before the company, which had done so well during the war, went under. After that I went to work for a good children's clothing company, but did not have a very lucrative territory, mostly Baltimore and Washington. I made some money, but not "real" money, as I had hoped. That would come later.

12. FAMILY, BUSINESS AND SUBURBAN LIFE

My life and work really only started to take shape once I got married, bought a house, and started my own business.

My marriage came about because in those postwar days, it was a valuable and comforting experience to visit with people from the same province in Germany. We had all lost so much that perhaps just being able to talk about life as it had been, and would never be again, provided some measure of continuity for us.

This was how I met my future wife, Lore. I was paying a visit to her parents, whom I had known back in Germany. They had owned a flour mill there, which they had lost and were now, it seemed, reëstablished in a new country with a new business.

The family had gotten out of Germany in 1937 and had come to New York with their seven-year old daughter, Lore. Needing some way of making a living, they started a cottage industry-type chocolate company, and sold their product door to door. They had done well during wartime because with food shortages, one could be sure to succeed at selling anything edible. We called those types of businesses "war babies."

When I reconnected with them, Lore was about 18 and was still in school. She was attractive to me, but when she got engaged, I simply assumed I was out of the running. A year or so later, though, I learned that the engagement was broken, and I asked her to marry me.

I cannot say that I had fallen madly in love with Lore. No, rather, it was that I felt it was just the right time to get married. I wanted to settle down and be an established, mature man with a wife and family. Lore accepted my proposal and in 1948, we got married in one of New York's largest synagogues.

Our wedding pictures are testimony to the lush and elegant affair that Lore's parents made to celebrate the occasion. You would never know from looking at the photos that all of us were refugees. We show all the signs of good, European breeding and pride.

My father-in-law and I are wearing top hats and tuxedoes, and look the very picture of wealth and comfort. My mother-in-law looks every bit the glamorous matron of the 1940s in a shimmering taffeta suit with a swirling confection of tulle atop her head. Lore is all in white, of course, her dark curls surrounding her sweet face. A lacy tiara and veil complete the virginal look required of a traditional bride.

We all appear very happy, but when I look at these photos now, I cannot help but think how innocent Lore and I were. I suppose one has to be

somewhat naïve in order to make such a leap of faith in life.

We took an apartment in Washington Heights, near my in-laws, until our brand new apartment in Queens was ready. Lore's father wanted me to come into his business, but something told me it was on the wane, and that this would not be a wise move for me. With the war years fading into history, this kind of small business was not bound to survive. It was good that I listened to this instinct, for the little chocolate company did go under and while I felt for my in-laws, I was to soon to discover the right path for myself.

Meanwhile, Lore got pregnant and nine months later, we had a perfect little baby girl. Of course, she brought a new element of joy to our lives. How could she not? We moved into that brand new apartment complex in Fresh Meadows, Queens, an area that was being developed for middle class, postwar families.

Now I knew I had to do something with myself, something original and creative. I realized that some people welcomed home shopping, what we would now call "personal shopping," so I started a business as a ready-to-wear and children's

clothing salesman. Focusing on the New York and Long Island communities, I brought the customer several styles and sizes to their home, and they could select whatever items they wanted from my stock. I was a one-man show, working at least 10-hour days and doing the bookkeeping at night. It was a tough struggle, but I survived and the business grew.

When our baby was one year old, we moved to a modest private house in a pastoral part of Queens. This turned out to be another smart choice, because the neighborhood remained stable for the subsequent decades, and I am still living there today.

At the time of this move, my business was growing slowly and then took a new turn. I was asked to come to a hospital in Rockaway to help a gentleman get some window shades. This small event changed the entire nature of my career.

Although I knew nothing about shades, I learned fast! I began installing and delivering them and the orders started to roll in. I decided to make a transition from children's clothing to industrial and home decorating — curtains, blinds and carpets. Teaching myself from books, I learned the methods for window treatment installations. I guess you could say I was doing my own "job training."

Soon I was able to take on customized orders. I became a specialist in supplying hospitals with both window and floor coverings, and mastered the art of making bedside curtains that provided patients with more privacy.

My business grew, and I benefited from the process of word of mouth recommendations that would result in more orders. I was conscious of my own intention to be honest, creative, friendly, reliable and innovative, for these were the qualities I had seen lacking in most contractors. On the practical side, I offered competitive prices to encourage people to do business with me.

Eventually, I phased out the private sales and turned more toward the commercial world. I obtained accounts with several hospitals, nursing homes, doctors' offices, some of New York's city and state buildings and the Navy. I became an expert on fire-rating standards and networked to provide up-to-date decorating ideas that were congruent with safety standards.

Working seven days a week, and long days at that, I made great connections, buying carpeting from the largest mill in Georgia and textiles from well known manufacturers on Long Island. I had relationships with the largest shipyards in the country.

In growing the business, I bought quantity orders of carpets, fabrics or tracks for the shipyard, and always managed to pay everything within 10 days, thus benefiting from a five percent discount. This helped with my reputation as an excellent customer. I felt that every dollar I saved was another dollar earned, a dollar in my pocket, not theirs.

Aside from my regular line of business with the hospitals and offices, I developed a line of curtains to be especially manufactured for Navy ships. The Navy would send me drawings and specifications and I'd make the curtains with tracks, according to their instructions. It was a unique service for which I had, in a sense, cornered the market. It was a great specialty and had to meet the Navy's specifications 100 percent, with no exceptions. If one did not deliver exactly what they had asked for, the job would be lost. The Navy had rules and regulations for everything from where the fabric had to be bought, which threads to use, how many stitches to the inch and even how the goods should be packed and sent.

Over time, I became one of the Navy's main suppliers of all types of curtains. I was able to bid on all contracts and since I had no overhead, I was able to land quite a few sizable ones. My accountant wanted me to incorporate, but I did not feel the need to. I was able to control my business on all ends: taking orders, delivering, installing, watching that payments arrived in time. While incorporating would have protected me, it also would have meant more taxation, forms, extra work. The wisdom of my decision all came together much later on for me when, in 2003, Northrop Grumman sent me a fax addressed to "Werner Kleeman, President, Werner Kleeman Company."

* * * * * * * *

Meanwhile, as this business was growing, life in the Navy changed in its style. Women came aboard and so the structure of the showers had to be modified. Suddenly, the Navy would purchase 100-150 shower curtains, all of which had to be flame retardant as well as able to ensure privacy. This was progress.

I received my payments on time; I could count exactly 30 days and a check would always arrive. This was an innovative, creative and honest business for me, and I became more prosperous. I never received any complaints that any item was not done to specification, and so I was known as a dependable vendor, which is precisely the reputation one wishes to establish in business.

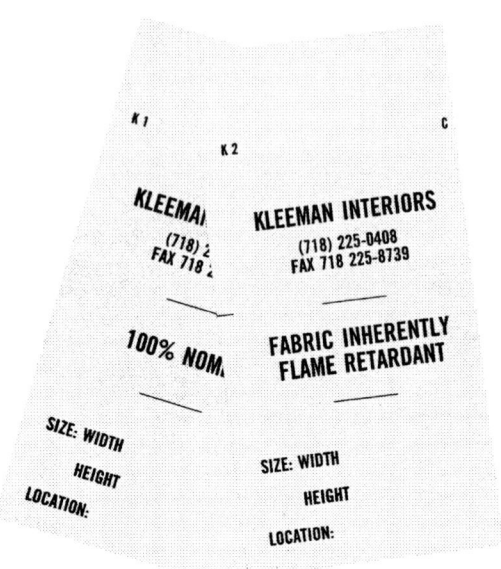

Because of my excellent credit rating, I was always able to get a discount on my bills. Driving myself, I always responded to the needs of all the hospitals, apartment houses and commercial offices I could contact. I used to call my business my "little gold mine."

I now had a foothold in the business world and this success fed my physical and mental stamina. I was able to work vigorous 18-hour days, and felt that I was liked and respected by all the people with whom I had dealings: the engineers, purchasing agents, doctors, nurses, real estate managers, administrators, and even housekeepers. With perseverance and ingenuity, my business savvy and my service-oriented nature, business blossomed. I felt proud to offer superior service.

After what I had seen in my first few jobs in the garment industry, I had a clear idea of what people needed if you expected to keep them as customers. Frequently, I would stop by to see clients without being asked, just to keep my face in their minds and have some cordial conversation. You cannot imagine how many times people would comment that it was just this face that they needed to see!

I also had very clear ideas about banks and how to deal with them, and my philosophy has not changed to this day. Some 40 years ago, Chemical Bank built a branch in my neighborhood. I immediately went there and opened a personal account as well as a business account. They were happy to have the business and waived all fees and expenses. And so it went for a long time.

But when managers change, there are always policy changes too. Back in about 1991, when Chemical merged with Chase Manhattan, I was told that I would have to pay various fees. I stood my ground and refused to allow them to force me into this new style of functioning. I simply told them I would not be burdened with these fees, most of which did not seem to be real anyway. And to this day I am still with them and have never paid a fee, unless of course it is a normal commission for the sale of stock.

*   *   *   *   *   *   *   *

During my years of hard work, Lore gave birth to another baby girl. Our daughters were a true delight to us. They were different from one another, yet they had a close bond that was easy to see and is still quite apparent today. We grew as a warm family.

In 1951, when I had first bought the house, we joined the Flushing Jewish Center in our neighborhood. We wanted to belong to some kind of Jewish community, and felt this was the best way to do it. My European background and upbringing aided me in making this decision, and I became active in the Jewish center, sending our daughters to the temple for their religious education. As a family, we attended services on the high holidays and sometimes on the Sabbath.

I became increasingly active in temple life and got involved in the affairs of my fellow congregants. There were quite a few members with backgrounds similar to mine, and they had settled in Flushing after the war. Some were the "elders," people in their 50s, who had started this congregation.

We always had strong leadership from the rabbis that we engaged. They were all graduates of Yeshiva University and often used our temple as a stepping stone to positions of greater responsibility. One particular rabbi stands out in my mind, though. Rabbi Paul L. Hait, a humble fellow, well educated and articulate. We had been able to woo him away from his congregation in New Orleans because he was a New Yorker who wanted to return to his hometown. His goal was to offer his children the opportunity to attend school in New York, and he was willing to sacrifice his post in New Orleans to provide this for them.

This rabbi became a cherished friend to my family. Over a period of about 20 years, he and his wife offered emotional support when we needed it the most. Since my wife suffered from depression and there was no effective help available, I relied upon the wisdom and compassion of both the rabbi and his wife. It was a blessing to have them nearby…..

I was also proud and happy for the rabbi when he achieved the position of Executive Director of the New York Board of Rabbis, a rank that brought honor and pride to Jewish life in New York. The mayor and Cardinal joined this illustrious man at various functions and were honored to sit on the dais with him.

I was elected Vice President of the synagogue and life there was vibrant and meaningful. But over time, the population of Flushing shifted. We lost members through attrition and migration to the suburbs. The newcomers to Flushing are mostly Asians, a rich blend of Chinese and Koreans. They are wonderful neighbors and friends. As a result of this shift, though, a few years ago, we found we were not able to get a minion for services, and we were forced to put the temple up for sale. It was sold within a few months and we moved our congregation to join the Fresh Meadows Jewish Center. We took everything we could with us, and found the move to be not only dramatic, but traumatic. It was one of those times in life when there is only one choice.

When I look back, I see that with the many activities of business family and suburban life, time flew by. My girls grew up quickly, or maybe it just seemed that way because we were all so busy. Before I knew it, they were out of high school and in college, one in Queens College and the other at SUNY Albany. They did well at school and I wanted to reward them. The best reward, I felt, was to guide them toward being as independent as possible. I gave each one a car so that they could travel back and forth from school freely and not have to depend on classmates for a lift. Of course, in those days there were no cell phones, in fact, there were not even any phones in the dorm rooms, so it was good to have my mind at ease, knowing my girls knew how to take care of themselves. Both daughters became fine women, wives and mothers, despite the fact that they did not grow up under perfect circumstances.

Unfortunately, after the birth of our second child, my wife had begun to suffer from a depression that did not seem to be connected to anything circumstantial. I have thought that her sadness might have always been there, hidden under the surface because she had left Germany as a child. She may not have known or understood the true depth of the tragedy that had befallen her family, but may somehow have internalized it. Although Lore's parents were able to leave Germany in 1937, her maternal grandparents were not. Trapped in the horrors of the Third Reich, they took their own lives. I never learned by what means Lore's mother found out that her parents were seen jumping to their deaths from a building. I have, however, conjectured that the grief that my mother-in-law experienced somehow seeped into her daughter's consciousness and marked her with a melancholia that only emerged in her adult life.

And so, woven into the years of work and raising children were the numerous futile attempts to get Lore the help she needed. No one, it seemed, could reach her. She spent years and years unable to participate fully in life, to enjoy the fruits of my hard work. As a committed husband, I did everything humanly possible to find the way for her to function, but I did not succeed.

Seeing that helping Lore was beyond my reach, I concentrated to the task of raising my two girls. I wanted them to have "normal" lives, not lives disrupted by family crises and emergency situations. My entire focus, for at least 20 years, was educating and bringing up my daughters while running my business. With my energy and drive, I was able to do this, but it came at a price. Lore passed away in the early 1980s, after many years of torment. I had not been able to find the remedy for her, but my conscience was clear, knowing I had tried every possible means.

My mother-in-law, Elisabeth, who had the misfortune of outliving her daughter, never really credited me for any of my efforts. This was no surprise, because she and I had not enjoyed a good relationship – it was always rather strained. In those days, not much was understood, much less known, about the nature of depression, and it was often believed that if one only had enough patience, one could reach the suffering victim. Elisabeth accused me of being short of patience with her daughter because sometimes when I was at my wits' end, I'd bring Lore back to her for a short stay. I needed a break from the relentless agony of trying to stave off yet another of Lore's suicide attempts. Elisabeth insinuated, and in not too subtle a manner, that these so-called suicidal episodes were really *my* attempts at murder! But I just I saw this as the result of her own lack of understanding of Lore's problem, combined with the weakly established relationship we had from the beginning of the marriage.

In family crises, as in all of life, one needs solid, trusting relationships, forged over time, that support the suffering family member, or members. I had never had that with my in-laws, so in this 20-year crisis, I had to go it alone. I did not let any of this bother me because my priority was my two daughters – I wanted to protect them and shield them from this ongoing tragedy. Although Elisabeth had no sympathy for me, or even for the girls, my daughters and I stayed close and took care of each other.

At the time of Lore's death, which was brought on by natural causes, the girls were already married and establishing their own lives. They would eventually have four wonderful children between the two of them. It was good to know I had provided for them and gave them the best possible guidance in life. Each girl had an elaborate, traditional Jewish wedding, and I had the honor of enjoying these affairs with some of those cherished military friends.

The photo shows the table in which all the army

buddies and their wives are joined. Because we were honoring the Fourth Division, I placed these guests at table number four.

From left to right, starting with the back row, they are: Mrs. Gatling, me, Judge Bailey, Colonel Gatling, Mrs. Keenan, John Keenan (Chief of Detectives of New York City and the only person here who is still alive); second row: Mrs. Melis, Joe Melis, Mrs. Johnson, Colonel Johnson (112th Infantry Regiment), Mrs. Harken, Mr. Harken of Port Washington. It makes me happy to think that all of us were able to be together for a happy occasion like this.

Today, when I see my daughters and grandchildren, I can say that it was all worth the effort, despite any difficulties or sadness that we may have endured.

* * * * * * * *

Once I was widowed, the business took on even greater importance, perhaps because my energy could be channeled completely toward the one goal. The tremendous growth of my company took about 30 years, which seemed to go very quickly. I suppose this was because I was working so feverishly that I was not aware of the passage

of time. My reputation was tops and all the responsibility for success or mistakes was mine, since I had always had done everything alone: ordering, delivering, installing, billing, collecting. One of the more practical keys to my success was to keep the business at home and never be burdened with overhead. This gave me the advantage of being able to bid low on large jobs that required three bids, such as hospital jobs. I had an excellent relationship with New York Health and Hospitals Corporation and stayed out of the way of union shops, which could make a small businessman's life complicated.

My house served me well in my life as a businessman. In fact, I still marvel at how compact and efficient the whole operation is. Besides providing me with comfortable living quarters, the house was and still is my office, which contains all my files and papers. The one-car garage is used for storing curtain rods and carpeting, and of course, my daughters' excess furniture that came home with them from college. No room for the car, but then, there is the driveway.

The basement has a special entrance in the rear of the house, which I use for storing tracks and equipment. I assemble them myself before sending them to the shipyard to be put on Navy ships. The basement is also the packing and shipping department. And of course, anyone who runs a business out of their home knows that these parts of the house can be written off for tax purposes.

Then there were the telephones. After I started the business, I had the telephone installed for work and personal life. I installed another line just for the girls so that they could call their friends. In those days, it was an innovation to make unlimited calls at a fixed rate — exactly what my teenage girls needed and loved. When they moved on to college, I appropriated their phone line for the fax, which was, at that time, a state of the art office tool. Like all small business owners, I found that a fax could greatly improve commerce. And I did all of this constructing, arranging and assembling myself, without bringing in extra help, which would have been costly. I have always felt good about my ability to manage and juggle all these aspects of the company, both cerebral and physical.

Once the girls were grown, I was able to focus on the business even more, devoting extra time to developing this company that I had started. Of course, I had my share of problems and learning experiences. In the early 80s it seemed that a trend of non-payment had appeared in the hospital world. Some invoices simply went unpaid, and in one case, when I had waited almost two years, I had to go to court.

Since I did not want to spend money on a lawyer, I presented all the information to the court, filling out a long form. The court set a date for a trial and on that day, the representative from the hospital did not show up. My case was transferred to an arbitrator who listened to the story. Ultimately, I was awarded a judgment against the hospital.

With this piece of paper in hand, I hired a city marshal to collect the money for me and he was successful. Check in hand, I walked into the bank. It had been a long journey, but a victorious one. This incident was not unique, but it stands out in my mind as the one requiring the most persistence.

And so the business went up and down, and suddenly I was 70! I realized that there was more to life than just working. I started to take more vacations, to travel, to expand my view. During this time, I became a grandfather, and this was another facet of life that brought me pleasure and satisfaction. Each of my daughters had a boy and girl, and all four grandchildren are just as wonderful as any grandparent could want them to be. During their early years, I wanted to be present when they took their first steps or tasted their first chocolate. I was always anxious to see them and hold those little babies, and as they grew, I delighted in their many accomplishments.

WERNER KLEEMAN
45-46 196TH PLACE
FLUSHING, N.Y. 11358

Tel: 718 225 0408
FAX 718 225 8739

412 523 -8596-
        7476

Account Number

ATT: GEORGE ANDREWS

Bill To: St. Lukes - Roosevelt Hospital
1000 Tenth Ave
New York, N.Y. 10019

ST. LUKE'S\ROOSEVELT
HOSPITAL CENTER
FAC. PLAN & CONST.
CONTRACTOR
WERNER KLEEMAN
Werner Kleeman
6/00

Invoice Date	Our Order No.	Your Order No.	Amount Due	
1/30/98	3135	1-1747694	1,297.—	✓
4/20/98	3175		1,652.—	✓
6/26/98	3205		60.—	✓
6/16/97	7025		75.—	✓
8/12/98	3240		150.—	✓
8/4/98	3231	1-0850228	295.—	X
2/26/99	3312		75.—	X
2/26/99	3313	1-1963429	450.—	X
3/1/99	3315	1-0964354	100.—	X Pd 8/24/01
10/5/99	3396	1-0971812	435.—	
10/5/99	3397	1-1972214	1,476.—	X
3/7/00	4127	R12702	492.—	
2/17/00	4112	1-1975134	400.—	X Pd 8/24/01
1/20/00	4114		285.—	X
1/11/00	4116		150.—	X
1/31/00	4245	R7761	4332.—	X Pd 8/24/01
4/20/00	4203	R25227	960.—	X Pd 8/20/01
4/6/00	4184		210.—	X
6/10/99	3387		46.80	X
			12,994.30	

Received 2/14/02

Current	30-60 Days	60-90 Days	Over 90 Days	Total

Deposit

As these children started to attend school, I offered to help with their education. I knew it would be easier for me to provide this than it would be for their parents. Over a period of several years, I wrote lots of checks to various universities and showed a real interest in the children's success. This was a genuine pleasure for me, and my family was most appreciative because during those college years, the average tuition was $35,000/year.

Then came some travel during school vacations and I was there with an open hand at all times. I shall always feel proud of myself that I was decisive and helped these children to develop their minds and to grow in their own way. I felt especially happy that I was able to contribute to something that I myself was deprived of.

13. A TURNING POINT

On a weekend at the end of May, 1984, I attended a mini-reunion of the Fourth Infantry Division in King of Prussia, Pennsylvania. I rode down with my friends, the Harkens, who were soldiers from the medical detachment.

During the afternoon, I noticed a nice young woman talking and interviewing soldiers. I had no idea what kind of information she was looking for, so I asked her what she was doing. She told me her name was Roberta Oster, and as we chatted, she noticed my German accent and started asking me some very pointed questions. She simply wanted to know everything about my life story. Since I was not in the habit of discussing it, I felt most uncomfortable.

Noticing this, Roberta led me into a private room and started what I considered to be an even tougher series of questions regarding my background, my stay in Dachau, my subsequent emigration from Germany, and how I had come to have the war experience I'd had. I did not really want to answer these inquiries, but Roberta persisted. The interview brought me to the edge of breaking down emotionally. She wanted to know if what I said I had experienced was the truth. She tested me, as if to imply that she was not sure I was actually Werner Kleeman, a D-Day veteran and member of the Fourth Division!

When she seemed convinced of my sincerity, she told me that she *needed* me because of my background and experience. She said she had never met a man who had actually come out of

Dachau, joined the Fourth Infantry Division and landed on D-Day in Normandy! She wanted to introduce me to Tom Brokaw for a special program that NBC was planning to air on June 6th, "D-Day Plus 40 Years."

Roberta pleaded with me to listen to her and accept this honor, and I replied that I would think over this opportunity once I had discussed it with my daughters. She said, should I decide to participate, I would have to come down to NBC Studios on the following Monday to meet with Mr. Brokaw. She told me that it was important for me to be there in person because if my personal story were included in Tom Brokaw's documentary, millions of viewers would learn the significance of D-Day in accelerating the end of the Holocaust. Also, Roberta confided that she, too, was Jewish and felt strongly that the story of D-day could not be told properly without mentioning the Holocaust. She was certain that Mr. Brokaw and the NBC viewers would be so moved to learn about a German-born man who had survived Dachau, went on to become an American soldier, landed in Europe on D-Day and ultimately arrested his former neighbors.

And so Roberta convinced me that the world needed to hear my story and thus, I decided to accept her invitation. I met Tom Brokaw, who interviewed me and agreed that I was the right person for this project. He took me around the NBC studios and introduced me to various staff members. I felt rather like a child on a school trip because they showed me a bit about how the evening news is produced and broadcast to the world. They even invited me to sit in Mr. Brokaw's chair.

It was a good thing that I had my passport handy and valid because within a few days I would be going to France to film the program at Utah Beach. NBC invited my older daughter Susan to come with me and she, too, had to make some quick arrangements, getting herself an emergency passport and enlisting her sister's cooperation in watching the children for that week.

When we landed in Paris, a limousine was waiting for us, ready to take us straight to Normandy. This journey, which had taken three months back in 1944, took just three hours in 1984. Our destination was Bayeux, near the Normandy coast, where NBC had booked accommodation at a chateau.

The next morning, another limousine came for us and took us to St. Marie DuMont to visit with the mayor. There we learned that the city officials had planned a reception and an elegant dinner for the participants.

The wonderful series of events for this project started that afternoon, when we went down to St. Mère Eglise. Back in my old terrain, I showed my daughter the church upon whose spire one of the wartime paratroopers had gotten stuck. Little by little, my own story, in its entirety, started to unfold for her. I had never really been able to tell my children what had happened during the war, and giving them the opportunity to see these places firsthand was invaluable. But even more would be revealed after the taping of the show.

We enjoyed lunch at the Café Steele in St. Mère Eglise, and then went down to the strip of sand called Utah Beach, which is now world famous. The area had been sealed off to the local people and only those participating in the filming had access to the area. The French police had secured it in preparation for the arrival of all the heads of state, who were coming for the anniversary ceremonies.

The day was windy and cold, and it was rather eerie to see the German bunkers in the beach wall. We couldn't really be sure that they were free of mines, either, and pondered whether there were still some that had not yet exploded. We did most of the filming on a boat that resembled the landing ship, which held about 30 soldiers.

With the filming done and all the requisite formalities and festivities accomplished, Susan and I left and continued our journey in another significant part of Europe. We flew to Frankfurt where we rented a car so that I could show her the town of Würzburg, where my grandparents lived before the Nazi takeover. I took her into the village and showed her where my family home had stood. We also looked for the Jewish cemetery in order to see if we could visit the graves of some of the relatives. Finding it was something of a struggle, because it was hidden and there was no one around to ask. But find it we did, and we spent a few solemn moments together, thinking of those who had departed so tragically.

In talking with various people in the village, I was able to find out the specific sad statistics about the fate of the Jews of my village. From 1936-1941, 35 people emigrated, going in various directions. The greatest number (23) went to the U.S.; three went to Palestine, three to England, five to South America and one to South Africa. Those were the lucky ones. An additional 32 were deported to the East, and none of them returned at the end of the war. There were also 36 soldiers from the village who lost their lives in combat. Knowing these numbers made the tragedy even more real.

Continuing our tour, I took Susan to see where her mother grew up and where her grandfather's flour mill had stood. Actually, the building that housed the mill was still standing. The sturdy brick factory building has a pointed roof and many large windows. At one end are two tall brick towers.

The setting is bucolic: the mill stands back from the road on a wide lawn and behind the building is the backdrop of a gently sloping green hillside. Evergreens and shrubbery grow on the land, making the whole scene rather peaceful. The building looks disused, which is just as well, for it harbors the memory of yet another family that had to leave behind an entire life, its livelihood and a vibrant business that was a source of work for many people before the war.

Next we went into Gaukönigshofen and met some of my family's former neighbors, who were farmers. Amazingly, they were still living in their house, just a couple of doors away from where we had lived. We all ate a bowl of soup together and chatted. It must have seemed strange to my daughter that I would even sit at the table with these people, and I sensed that she was uncomfortable. Still, we were experiencing something important together.

* * * * * * * *

We returned home, and on June 6th, the program we had filmed was aired. A group of us, friends and family, watched it together in the living room.

Of course, we had no idea what would actually be shown. (Curiously, the rabbi at my synagogue refused to announce this broadcast to the congregation. It happened to fall on Shavuous, and he did not wish to encourage people to participate in this activity on a holiday.)

After the broadcast, phone calls started to come in from all over. One was from the boys who ran the ship LST 282, which was bombed and sank while on a mission in the Mediterranean. Subsequently, these fellows tracked me down and made me an "honorary member" of their group, the US Landing Ship Tank Association. They used to meet once every other year, and I later attended several of their reunions. I always felt very respected and accepted and enjoyed the fellowship of the group.

The trip to Normandy was a most unusual experience. Tom Brokaw later met with a few of the soldiers who had been part of the D-Day invasion. He told them that the whole experience shook him. It apparently awakened him to what had really gone on, and inspired him to gather all his thoughts and put them down on paper. He wrote a masterful book, "The Greatest

Generation," which stayed on the best seller list for months. Tom became active in the pro-veteran groups and contributed highly to the founding of the Eisenhower Museum in New Orleans.

Some time after the trip, a package from Tom arrived. Inside was a sporty, smart, navy blue jacket with red piping. A letter enclosed in the package read:

Below, in his own handwriting, it reads, *"Werner, I hope you had a good trip to your home village,"* which is perhaps the most touching part of the letter.

Another document that nicely recaps all of this is an article that came out in a German newspaper several years later. Somewhat of a story within a story, the article fills in some of the gaps I have not covered in this memoir:

From the *Würzburger Zeitung*, January 3, 1987:

Werner Kleeman, the Reluctant Traveler

Kleemann, born in 1919 in Gaukönigshofen, the son of a Jewish grain merchant, grew up in a so-called castle. In the 19th century, this building belonged to the famous Jewish family, the Hirsches, whose members received honorary titles from King Ludwig I for their

NBC News A Division of National Broadcasting Company, Inc.   Thirty Rockefeller Plaza New York, N.Y. 10020   212-664-4214

Tom Brokaw

June 28, 1984

Mr. Werner Kleeman
45-46 196th Place
Flushing, New York 11358

Dear Mr. Kleeman:

Please accept this jacket as a small token of our appreciation for your participation in D-Day Plus Forty. As I hope you already know, it was a triumph for NBC News. You and the other veterans who participated can take full credit.

On a personal note, it was an honor for me to be with you in Normandy. I was touched by your modesty and your continuing commitment to the values for which you fought 40 years ago. In the course of my work I meet the rich and the famous but I can honestly say I've never met a more impressive group than the one assembled for D-Day Plus Fourty.

Thank you for the privilege of sharing that important time in your life.

Sincerely,

Tom

TB:amw
Enclosure

Werner - I hope you had a good trip to your home village.

participation in the economic development of Bavaria.

While Werner was attending the Oberrealschule in Würzburg from 1930 - 1933, he visited his father during sessions at the market exchange.

Finally to England

In 1937, after the Nazi regime had been in power for 4 years, Kleemann decided to immigrate to the USA, since other plans to immigrate to Palestine, as his brother had, were hopeless. In January, 1939, he succeeded in reaching England for a temporary stay and also arranged for his parents and brother and sister to get there. By December he reached New York. Less than three years later, Kleemann, who dropped one letter from his name to Americanize it, obtained US citizenship.

"In 1942, I was drafted into the army," Kleeman remembers on a visit to Würzburg. "One could not volunteer for the service, but had to wait until called up in the draft. After receiving three months' basic training, one was sworn in as an American citizen. Henry Kissinger, who was from Furth, went through the same process...."

The Fourth American Infantry Division and Werner Kleeman being assigned to it, were selected to participate in the Allied invasion of Europe. In 1943, he had already done maneuvers for this in Florida before the troops embarked for England. "It was a very dangerous crossing," Kleeman said. "The Germans tried to sink every ship with their submarines. In the south of England, in the vicinity of Exeter, the soldiers practiced for the invasions during the following months, never knowing where the invasion was to take place."

During one of these large scale maneuvers, German E-boats sank two American ships. Nine hundred soldiers lost their lives. In return, the Allied forces shot down a German airplane. When the pilot was pulled out of the burning plane, Kleeman interrogated him and found out that he had taken off from Giebelstadt, which was about two miles from Gaukönigshofen.

In England, Kleeman, who was appointed Interpreter in the Division Headquarters, acquainted himself with a young man by the name of Jerome David Salinger, who worked for the Counter Intelligence Department and later became famous for his novel <u>The Catcher in the Rye</u>. *Later on, Ernest Hemingway arrived to join the troops as war correspondent. The three men spent evenings together. Kleeman was told by Hemingway that during the 1920s, he was often a visitor to*

Würzburg and remembered well the delicious trout that he ate there.

Early in the morning of June 6th, the delayed invasion started. At 5 o'clock, when Werner Kleeman reached the beach on the Normandy coast area called "Utah Beach," the Allied troops had already advanced a few kilometers inland. On September12th, 1944, the immigrant was part of the first group of American soldiers to walk on German soil in the Eifel. "Nearby, we saw the dragon's teeth of the Siegfried Line. Several weeks later, the Division suffered heavy casualties during the counter offensive in the Ardennes. Afterwards, it moved through Worms into Baden and conquered Tauberbiscohsheim, Roettingen, Bad Mergentheim and Rothenburg."

In the summer of 1945, Kleeman arranged to be stationed with the military government in Ochsenfurt. His knowledge of the district helped him to get important assignments besides his job an interpreter, to examine and analyze the large industrial companies in the district. Afterwards, he arranged for the arrest of all men who started out from Ochsenfurt during November of 1938 to destroy the property of all Jews and were responsible for his arrest and his having been sent to Dachau. An old acquaintance signaled to him.

"Your presence here is dangerous and someone might want to harm you." Upon hearing this, he lived very cautiously and did not dare to go out after dark any longer. He posted guards at his office so he could sleep nights.

A few months later, Werner Kleeman returned to the USA and started civilian life again. In 1948, he married an immigrant from lower Frankonia. In 1984, American television produced a detailed program about Kleeman's experiences from Dachau to Utah Beach. Today, Würzburg and Caen are cities of partnership and in Normandy, the foundation stone was laid down for a museum dedicated to the invasion and subsequent peace. In Gaukönigshofen, they plan to restore the synagogue again. And Werner Kleeman needs less than 24 hours to return from a visit to Würzburg to New York again. "Times have changed," he wrote in a letter.

*   *   *   *   *   *   *   *

There is one more story in connection with the D Day Plus Forty experience. In September, 1998, I received an invitation from Community School Board 20, in Brooklyn, to attend an affair commemorating *Kristallnacht*. It would be held on the 10th of November, the actual anniversary date of that horrific event.

For this affair, I was asked to furnish a tape of the "D-Day Plus Forty" broadcast. I asked my daughters to accompany me that night, as I thought they might learn something of value.

The invitation stated that a German consul and Theodore Roosevelt IV would be attending as a guest speaker. I tied this Roosevelt to the General Roosevelt who had served in the Fourth Infantry Division on D-Day back in 1944. My hunch was correct.

When approaching Mr. Roosevelt, I opened a bag of books I had with me and took one out. On page two of one of the books, there was a photo of his grandfather dressed as a Brigadier General with the Fourth Infantry Division. He was so shocked

and surprised to see this and to see all of the books that I was carrying with me that night. One was the story of D-Day at Utah Beach and another was a history of the Fourth Infantry Division during WWII. Apart from the wonderful photos in the books, there was also the text of the Congressional Medal of Honor that was awarded posthumously to General Roosevelt. I promised to send Mr. Roosevelt a copy of each book. He was quite shaken to see such valuable materials and information 50 years after his grandfather had passed away, and was especially touched because he had never met his grandfather.

Later on, in 1999, when I turned 80, I invited Mr. Roosevelt to the grand party that my daughters threw for me. He was not able to attend, but he did send a very cordial, warm letter, which I have always cherished.

The very next year, when the new Eisenhower Museum was built in New Orleans and was awaiting its dedication, I arranged to have an invitation sent to Mr. Roosevelt. He was honored and accepted the invitation. I traveled to New Orleans with one of my daughters and two grandchildren with the intention of exposing them to history in the making.

Everything went as I had hoped. We all ate breakfast with Mr. Roosevelt and participated in a film focusing on the event.

I sat in the coliseum during the afternoon next to Mr. Roosevelt. Secretary of Defense William Cohen, who delivered a memorable speech, did not know that this grandson of the Brigadier General was in the audience when he made these closing remarks:

"...*the oldest soldier to land in the first wave on that day was Brigadier General Theodore Roosevelt, Jr. And as he stood on that beach in mid-century, he may have recalled his father's words at the optimistic dawn of the 1900s. He said, 'Greet the new century high of heart, and face the mighty task which the coming years will surely bring.' So today we're greeting a new century and dedicating this hall of heroes. To us falls the challenge to go forward with high hearts, prepared to meet the mighty tasks of tomorrow, and to recall with grateful hearts the noble men who carried the world across that long and now sacred strip of shore. Let us say thank you very much.*"

In 2004, the 60th anniversary of D-Day, Ted Roosevelt traveled to Paris and Normandy with his wife and son and I went with Major Fiset and my two daughters. We all met at the Café Roosevelt, which is now a landmark at Utah Beach in Normandy. All of these events that included Mr. Roosevelt are among my fondest, for they connect my present with my past.

At the newly opened Café Roosevelt, there was an opportunity for the D-Day veterans to sign in. The photo shows the Honor Board, which bears our signatures.

During this trip we also went to Würzburg, where we were invited to visit with the mayor. The next photo shows Major Fiset, then age 92, me, age 85, and Dr. Adolf Bauer, the Second Bürgermeister.

AMERICAN FORCES INFORMATION SERVICE
DEFENSE VIEWPOINT

National D-Day Museum Opening, Public Celebration

Remarks as Delivered by Secretary of Defense William S. Cohen, New Orleans Arena, New Orleans, Louisiana, Tuesday, June 6, 2000

Tom [Brokaw], thank you very much. Distinguished guests, ladies and gentlemen.

Last evening, Janet [Cohen] and I had the opportunity to stop by Brennan's Restaurant to pay tribute and say thanks to so many in this city and elsewhere who have made these two days possible. I commented at that time, paraphrasing Thackeray, that New Orleans is the city where you can eat the most, drink the most and suffer the least. [Laughter] And I would like to add for the past two days that New Orleans has been the city where I have spoken the most, and I hope you have suffered the least. [Laughter and applause.]

I can't tell you what it was like to be in that audience today, in that parade, as I watched all of those men and women march by, and the feeling that I had deep in my heart. I did a number of interviews during the course of the last two days, and each time a reporter would say, "What is the significance of this museum?" The short answer is, it forces us to pause and to reflect about the meaning of who we are and what we've done and what we're going to do tomorrow.

If you look at the futurists like Alvin Toffler who about 30 years ago said that we were living in a time of future shock, a time when events were going to speed up time itself, and that our values and our customs and our traditions would be shaken in the hurricane winds of change. And I think all of us have come to appreciate how technology has actually miniaturized the world. The world today is not much bigger than a ball spinning on the finger of science.

But we also know that technology is neutral. It can be used for good or evil. It was Winston Churchill who reminded us of this in that great Iron Curtain speech that he gave so many years ago when he said that, "We can return to the Stone Age on the gleaming wings of science." So what is really important as we rocket our way into the future is the preservation of our values.

I had a professor once who said that ideals without technology is a mess, but technology and technique without ideals is a menace. That's really what is at the heart of this new museum, to capture our ideals and our values.

I couldn't help but be struck last evening in watching "The Shooting War" produced by Richard Schickel and also be mindful of Steven Spielberg's "Saving Private Ryan," that how absolutely random war is; why so many died, and so many others lived.

I think it was Patton who said, "Let us not ask God why young men such as these should die in war. Let us rather thank God that such men lived." Without them, we would be living in a very different world. [Applause.] These men and women gave so much for us so that we could be here gathered in this wonderful arena to celebrate life and the future.

But I recall the words of Elie Wiesel who was a young boy then. He was waiting behind that Atlantic Wall, unaware that his liberators were jumping through that eerie dawn. Wiesel years later offered this thought.

He said, "A museum is a place where we should feel united in memory." And that's what I felt today. That's what I feel when I look at all of the men and women who have served us, all of our heroes, that I feel united in memory. That's the essence of what this museum is going to represent.

I'd like to close with thanks, first of all, to President Clinton for giving me the opportunity to serve in the greatest capacity that one could ever hope to achieve, to represent the men and women in uniform all across our country, who are scattered all across the globe. He has given me and Janet an opportunity to serve and to say that when it comes to national security there are no politics involved. There are no Republicans or Democrats or Independents. There is only one America for all of us in service. (Applause.)

I would like to close with noting that the oldest soldier to land in the first wave on that day was Brigadier General Theodore Roosevelt, Jr. And as he stood on that beach in mid-century he may have recalled his father's words at the optimistic dawn of the 1900s. He said, "Greet the new century high of heart, and face the might task which the coming years will surely bring."

So today we're greeting a new century and dedicating this hall of heroes. To us falls the challenge to go forward with high hearts, prepared to meet the might tasks of tomorrow, and to recall with grateful hearts noble men who carried the world across that long and now sacred slip of shore. Let us say thank you very much. [Applause.]

13. A RESPITE FROM WORK

I had worked hard for many years and I knew I needed to balance out this intensive lifestyle. Since the down time for my business was mid-December till early January, I decided to use this period each year to travel.

My first regular destination was Israel, where I visited my brother and a handful of cousins with whom I enjoyed a warm relationship. Being Jews in the Diaspora, we all enjoyed reconnecting and feeling some of what we had known in the years before the events of the war separated us.

On my way back home, I often made a stop in Europe, usually in Switzerland or Germany. There was a spa in Zurzach, Switzerland, where I looked forward to taking the thermal water treatment before returning to the bleakness and darkness of the New York winter, where I would resume work.

On one of these stays at the spa, I made the acquaintance of the manager, with whom I had some interesting and revealing conversations. He had made some observations during the war that he recounted to me. He said that back during those years, day after day and night after night, trains loaded with German soldiers used to travel across the Swiss rails into Italy. In Italy, the trains were routed to ports for reloading and shipping their goods to Africa. This daily routine was characterized by a request to the Germans to lower the shades of the train windows while passing through Switzerland so that the local people could not see what was going on.

This was a disturbing revelation and food for thought. The Swiss, who always prided themselves on being "neutral," were allowing Germans to travel through their land with soldiers and confiscated goods. This cost the Allies untold sacrifices of soldiers in both Africa and Italy. When I see photos of military cemeteries in Africa or Sicily, I ask myself how many soldiers died because of the help of the Swiss in the German war effort. I ask myself, where was the American ambassador? Why was this hypocrisy tolerated?

Of course, the Swiss knew that Americans would never bomb the railways of a sacred space like Switzerland! No doubt, the German government had a secret treaty with the Swiss government that allowed it to carry on this operation. But then, nothing is surprising about the actions of the Swiss people. Their behavior with deposits in their banks speaks loudly and clearly: they aided and abetted Germans who stole everything from Jews and then exterminated them. It is a small consolation, but in the past few years, the Swiss have been forced to open their books, so to speak, and show how much money was hidden in their banks.

This topic brings up many emotions, but these thoughts are really all part of the experience of having lived through many decades subsequent to the war. Work, family, travel, and cultivating relationships: these are the elements that filled many of those decades.

* * * * * * * *

People have often wondered why the story of my life does not include a great romance, and I have been criticized for not inventing one for this memoir! While I agree that passionate love and romance are surely something worth pursuing, my life was structured in such a way that I was not destined to enjoy either of these. I have emphasized again and again that I had to choose many times to make my daughters the greatest priority in my life, and I do not regret doing that.

Of course, as a widower in New York City, and one of good means and good breeding, I was the object of many women's affections – some sincere and some not so sincere. Among these, there were various romances, but none of enduring quality. Given the kinds of good quality relationships I had had with people in business, military and community life, I would not hold in high esteem any romantic relationship that was nothing more than trivial companionship.

However, I will highlight one of these romances, simply to illustrate the role it played in contrast to more significant pursuits. It was a relationship that made even more salient the value I place on relationships and experiences that are solid and durable.

In 1990, when I had been widowed for more than a decade, I met Helga Stern, a widow living near me in Flushing. We met casually at the bank one day and, learning that we lived just 10 blocks from one another, we started seeing each other.

There were some similarities in our backgrounds – we were both German Jews whose families had been forced to leave their homes. This made it comfortable for us to be together, to speak and share ideas, since we had a common upbringing and had suffered a common fate.

Helga used to come over every evening after work and prepare supper for me and we would dine together. It was relationship of convenience that served both of us, furnishing us with adult companionship on several levels. While there was neither a spiritual or physical bond between us, it was nice for each of us to have a "boyfriend" and "girlfriend" (for lack of better terms) late in life. But it was not destined to last very long.

Helga had a son and daughter and a few grandchildren. I did not know them or learn much about them at first, but the stories buried in the family would emerge as the relationship progressed. During the summer of 1990, when we traveled together to Tacoma to visit Helga's son, Steven, and his family, I would learn of some of the peculiarities that existed in this family….

Before we made the trip, I had written to Steven to give him the heads up, so to speak, that I would be traveling with his mother. In my letter, I alluded to the fact that we were having a romantic relationship and asked, in a subtle way, if this presented any kind of a problem in his household. I received a warm letter in return, but this warmth, I later learned, was deceptive. Perhaps Steven had no objection to his mother and me being a couple under his roof, but I did meet with some resistance from his wife. The letter reads as follows:

March 6, 1990

Dear Werner,

I appreciate your letter of February 22, 1990. Though I feel there was no need for you to write it, that you did shows that you are a caring person. As you probably know from my mother, my family is the most important thing in the world to me. Anything that affects them I take a great interest in. You will see that this summer when you meet Faith, Glenn, Kelly, and Ben.

As for the relationship you and my mother have developed, I believe that the two of you are both worldly and mature adults. Any decision the two of you make will be honored, as I have said to my mother. Please take good care of her. I look forward to meeting you this summer.

Sincerely,

Mark Stern

When we arrived at Steven's house, though, the tone was somewhat different. I was assigned a room in the basement, as the couple, evidently, did not want their children to see their worldly and mature grandmother sleeping in the same room with me. This I could live with.

Then I was told that Steven's wife was a very strict Lutheran and that the children had been brought up in that faith. Nothing wrong with that, I thought, until I learned that these children had not been told that their own father was Jewish, and *certainly* had not been told what had happened to their paternal grandparents and extended family back during the war. This had all been kept a secret from Steven's children and perhaps from his wife as well. This was disturbing to me, for I have been railing against this kind of deliberate ignorance since I left Europe. But it was not mine to object to; I was in the home of people I probably would never see again. Still, I did not understand Helga allowing this myth to persist. What did the children think about their father? Who was he? Where did he come from? And what would explain this German grandmother in their midst?

The next day, after our brief visit, I rented a car and we drove to Seattle, where I had a cousin I had not seen since leaving Germany in 1939. Cousin Laura and I were related through our mothers, who were sisters. Laura's parents had a department store back in Germany, but like so many Jews, they were forced to leave everything behind to save their own lives.

It is a story that is worthy of a whole book of its own. Laura's husband, my cousin, had come to the U.S. before the war to get an affidavit to immigrate. But while he was here, the war broke out. He went back to Europe to get his family out and got "stuck" there. Very late in the war, around 1941, he was able to get himself, his wife and their two children out of Germany, but they all had to go via Poland, Russia and Japan. Ultimately, when they crossed the Pacific and arrived on American soil, my cousin felt that they had all traveled enough and simply settled on the west coast. That is how one Jewish family came to settle in Seattle.

When I visited them with Helga, all of us went out for a very memorable seafood dinner. Of course, the talk turned to old times, both good and bad. It was not a long visit, but long overdue. But then I had to move on to one more person whom I wanted to see.

Irving Wirth was a psychiatrist who came from my village in Germany. He was very happy that I had contacted him and we arranged to meet for breakfast the next morning. At breakfast I gave him a copy of a book *Die Juden in Gaukönigshofen* (more on this in chapter 16), by Dr. Thomas Michel. This was a comprehensive study of the history of our hometown and to Irving, it was a miracle. In the book was the story of his grandfather, as well as other information that both shocked and delighted him. His interest and his reaction alone made the trip worthwhile.

Helga and I traveled well together on that journey, and so we planned another one in 1992. This may have proved to be a mistake, but one can rarely see these things in advance, and if we do, we ignore the signals. The purpose of the next trip was to see Alaska and go fishing for salmon.

This had long been a dream of mine and now I was going to make it come true.

I had done some fishing on Long Island, where once a year I'd take a charter boat out on the ocean with the other deep sea fishermen. The catch was never great but the experience was wonderful. A trip to Alaska to go salmon fishing is something every fisherman wants and so I made plans to go in July of that year. Helga wanted to come along and I could not refuse, although this was not the way I had envisioned this trip.

When I went to pick Helga up to go to the airport, I found she had packed way too much clothing – it looked as though we were going away for a month! I became furious, saying things I should not have, alluding to her staying home and not making the trip with me. She cooperated, though, and re-packed, using two smaller suitcases, but did reproach me for criticizing her. She said that if I did not like the way she packed, I should have bought her the correct luggage. It was a silly quarrel, symptomatic, perhaps, of my underlying resentment at wanting to go to Alaska alone.

Ironically, after rushing to the airport, we found we had to sit there for five hours because of an accident that occurred between two planes. We arrived late in Salt Lake City, missing our connection to Anchorage, and had to spend the night there.

Finally, one day late, we arrived at our destination and checked into a motel. I rented a car and we did a little sightseeing around the island. The countryside was lovely, as I had imagined it would be, but I knew that my real goal was to get to the fishing.

The next day I engaged a guide to take me fishing and make all the necessary arrangements. I had to buy a license and a ticket to board the fishing boat, and did everything with the expectation that Helga would be otherwise occupied during my expedition.

But when Helga learned that I had made all the arrangements for myself alone, she was livid. She said that she, too, wanted to have a fishing experience, and how could I think of doing this without her? I explained that this was something I was looking forward to and had envisioned it in a particular way. My vision did not include baiting hooks for her or becoming distracted in any way by another person for whom I was responsible. I reminded her that when I first announced that I was taking this trip, I told her that I intended to go alone. It was she who had insisted upon accompanying me, and now this was the disastrous result.

I suppose it is not the first time a man has wanted to have a solo experience at a sport without the benefit of female company. Perhaps if it had not been my first time, I might have been willing to modify my plans, but I stood my ground, making Helga even angrier. She threatened to leave then and there, and I told her she could do that. She did not, in fact, leave, but this was the beginning of the downfall of the relationship.

I had my fishing experience and caught five beautiful salmon that day, the maximum that is permitted for one fisherman. I took the fish to a smoke house and had them smoked and packed to bring back. Once home, I gave the fish to my family and friends, all of whom agreed that one has to taste something this unique and wonderful to appreciate it.

A picture from this trip shows me in my navy blue "D Day Plus Forty" bomber jacket that Tom Brokaw gave me. More important, though, are the magnificent salmon hanging in the background!

The next two photos show the rest of the fishermen and the catch. When seen in color, these photos convey the silver sky and crisp air of the Alaskan experience.

The fishing was a success, but the relationship between Helga and me failed. The trip awakened some bitter feelings between us, feelings that did not dissipate when we returned to New York. She started to voice various complaints, among them that I was paying too much attention to my children and grandchildren. There is nothing more hurtful that she could have said, and with this, I knew the

relationship was coming to its end. Nonetheless, within a few months, she demanded that I take her on vacation – I suppose she thought I owed her something for what had happened in Alaska. I did not want to go on vacation, though, and told her that I had business to attend to, which was true. And with this, she packed whatever items she was keeping at my house and said goodbye.

I felt a great wave of relief when she walked out of my life. I never called her again, never looked for her, and have no regrets about the end of this affair. I learned once again, as I had with other choices I had to make in my life, that my children and their children come first. How can one regret a choice such as that?

14. A POSTWAR FRIENDSHIP - JOHN GROTH

Suddenly, I was 82 and it was time to slow down and reflect on all that had happened thus far. I now turn back to one of the salient characters in my life, and a relationship that I cherished.

My treasured comradeship with the artist John Groth grew as a result of a succession of several events after the war. Our friendship and his art, too, grew visible in a number of interesting ways.

The inception of our acquaintance took place early in the war, when we were first on our way to Cherbourg, the first large city to be liberated. We had taken a prisoner named Leo Hammes and, in a circuitous route, Hammes played an important role in Groth becoming a well known artist.

Hammes, who was from Bleialf, Germany, that sleepy village near the Belgian border, was captured on day 18 of the American invasion. After he was processed as a prisoner of war, he was shipped to England and from there, to the U.S. He ended up in Fort Benjamin Harrison, Indiana, and remained there as a war prisoner until his return to Germany sometime in 1948.

During November, 1944, Hammes got a Chicago publication, *Parade Magazine*. While reading it, he came across a double-page spread of the drawings of his hometown, which had been done by this soon-to-be-famous war artist.

Somehow, this article found its way into the hands of a gentleman who, many years later, came into Bleialf. He was interested in the history of the town and was searching for details about the fighting during WWII. He had gotten hold of that issue of *Parade* from Hammes, and had been studying it. Driven by curiosity, he wrote to the German consul in New York and the American consul in Stuttgart to find out more about this article. Then he wrote (in German) to the artist, in New York. Groth, not able to read the letter, contacted me and asked me to translate it for him. Thus began our friendship, a mail and phone correspondence, which developed into an in-person relationship that was very dear to me.

In the postwar years, John would make a habit of

calling me to announce a trip he was taking, such as for the Marine Corps, to Vietnam or for a sporting event in India. He always found time to let me know when he was to leave town. War sketches and sporting events were his expertise and WWII had offered him plenty of opportunities to witness certain battles. He managed to be up front where the action was.

During the war, John was one of the first reporters to enter Paris, and he and Ernest Hemingway located Pablo Picasso, who had stayed in Paris at that time. When Picasso and Groth first met, they sketched portraits of one another. Groth gave his sketch to Picasso, but Picasso gave Groth his agent's business card, indicating that Groth would have to pay for the sketch. I don't believe he ever followed up, but today that sketch would be worth millions!

John and I corresponded back and forth, exchanging experiences, and sometimes we would meet for dinner. About that time, I was President of the New York/New Jersey chapter of the Fourth Infantry Division Association. On the first Tuesday of each month, we used to meet at the Tough Club, located at what was then a very prestigious New York address: 14th Street between Seventh and Eighth Avenues. It was one of the oldest clubs in the city, where many judges and politicians were members, and one might run into notable figures like Carmine DeSapio. The club was closed to members on Tuesdays, making it possible for our chapter to meet there. The meals were excellent and very reasonable, and the drinks were man-sized, so John and I often met there for our ritual dinner. In this venue, our friendship had a chance to blossom.

*   *   *   *   *   *   *   *

Apart from my burgeoning relationship with my artist friend, there are other nice memories associated with that period of my life. In 1973, the association invited the mayor of Ste. Marie DuMont, Michel de Vallavielle, and his wife to come to New York for a two-week visit, as our guests. We put the couple up at the Westbury Hotel, a small, intimate hotel that had been frequented by President Kennedy. Before they arrived, I contacted the French consulate in New York and asked that they arrange a party in honor of the visit. They agreed, and date was set for a Monday evening at 5PM.

> JOHN GROTH
> 61 EAST 57TH STREET
> NEW YORK, N.Y. 10022
> 212 355-0284
>
> oct 14,
>
> Dear Werner, nice to hear from you, and good to hear that Louis Fiset is coming to New York! — He's going for a ten day stint, to North Carolina on oct 18 — and the only free lunch day I've got while he is here is Wednesday oct 17. — I lunch with a few friends — in communications and are interested in the outdoors, fishing, etc. — we meet at the Overseas press club in the Chemists club Bldg. at 52 East 41, street between Madison and Park avenues. If it doesn't interfere with your plans for Louis — give me a call about 11:30 a.m. on Tuesday —

The consul was in France, so the deputy consul was in charge. The consulate allowed us to invite 40 guests, which I selected from the association. Our lead man was Colonel Gatling, since he had been a senior officer. The reception went well and afterwards, we took the mayor and his wife to the well known French restaurant, La Caravelle, where our host, Mr. Soltner, was happy to serve us his best.

I met with French dignitaries and when, a few weeks later, the Second French Armored Division came to New York, I was invited to attend their festivities at the Waldorf. About 1,000 people were present in the magnificent ballroom, and it was there that I received great recognition: the French *Croix de Guerre*.

I alerted the Consul General of France that we had had this affair, and shortly after that, I received a letter from him thanking me for our efforts.

* * * * * * * *

About 20 years later, I received an invitation from the French consul in New York to attend a reception at the consulate. The event centered on my receiving yet another honor, the Liberation Medal, commemorating the liberation of Paris in August, 1944.

Unfortunately, I was out of town that week, and so I asked my good friend, John Keenan, to attend and represent me. He did, and he also received this same medal.

In honor of the Hon. Mayor of Sainte Marie du Mont & Madame Michel de Vallavieille

Le Consul Général de France a.i.

prie
Mr. & Mrs. Werner Kleeman
de lui faire l'honneur
to come to a reception
le Monday, August 6 at 6 pm.

R.S.V.P. 934 Fifth Avenue
LE 5-0100 New York, N.Y. 10021

* * * * * * * *

I now return to thoughts of my friend, John Groth, and our evolving friendship. John belonged to the Overseas Press Club, which later merged with the Chemists' Club and we made a habit of meeting there occasionally. Our lives and values were quite different. John was a city-dweller with an apartment on East 57th Street. He had had four marriages, and had led his life in a very "bohemian" fashion, as befitted a New York artist. His office, if you could call it that, was also on East 57th Street, and was the size of a closet.

LE CONSUL GÉNÉRAL DE FRANCE
A NEW-YORK

934 FIFTH AVENUE
NEW YORK, N.Y. 10021

September 12, 1973

Dear Mr. Kleeman:

    I wish to thank you for your letter of August 13 which I found upon my return to New York.

    I am extremely pleased to learn that the visit of Mayor Michel de VALLAVIELLE and wife to the United States was a success thanks to the Veterans of the 4th Infantry Division.

    Thanking you again for all you did to make the stay of my compatriots in New York a very pleasant one, I remain

Very sincerely yours,

Gérard GAUSSEN
Consul General of France

Mr. Werner KLEEMAN
45-46 196th Place
Flushing, N.Y. 11358

It was both exciting and heartwarming to be John's friend. He used to send me a special drawing every year, around the Christmas season. I, in turn, always sent him a Christmas card. I usually tucked the drawings away, hoping to one day sort them out and start taking better care of them. *The New York Times* used to print one every week and I saved most of them. *The New Yorker*, *Holiday Magazine* (a publication for travelers) as well as other publications, also used John's drawings.

Time went by and John moved to a two-room apartment on East 86th Street. When I went to pay him a visit in his new surroundings, I found him aching and complaining about not feeling well at times. But he had created a cozy little homestead for himself, where he lived very simply.

There was a bed in the corner of the suite; his files, drawing table and some other equipment filled the two rooms. There was a little burner to warm up food. Some of his female art students lived in the building and they looked after him.

During our visits, we would pass the time gossiping and reminiscing about our days together in Europe. Once when I left, he gave me some drawings of the evacuation in Bleialf during the war, which brought back such vivid memories.

The last time I saw John was in 1987. In March of that year, I had the mayor of my hometown come to New York for two weeks and I arranged with the German consulate to have a reception in his honor. I planned a cocktail party for 40 guests with snacks and lots of German wine. Of course, John was among the guests. I also asked J.D. Salinger, who, being the colorful character that he was, called the consul and wanted to know why he was invited. I guess he decided not to attend, but John did show up. He sat at a table next to Izz Goldstein, a Fourth Division man, and I noticed that the two had a good rapport with one another. John handed out notices that night about his move uptown. He gave one to Izz, as well as Bob Boyer and Peter Dunsay, engineers who were building a hospital. Bob and Peter had no idea who John was but I wanted them to save this little piece of paper, knowing that some day it would be worth something. I always felt that John's notoriety would come in time.

Some nice relationships were formed as a result of

Diary — Ron Alexander

Sketchbook

They ordered freely: smoked salmon, foie gras, a ...

this social event. Izz later became a friend of Hemingway and subsequently got a Christmas card from him every year. I have always felt that this event was not just a cocktail party. It was a friendly mixture of New York people, all connecting with one another.

The following year, I read John's obituary in the Times. My sadness and sense of loss were mixed with the gratitude I felt when I saw my name was listed as one of his personal friends. I think I had not known, until I read that obituary, that I was considered a special friend. I did not realize that we were that close or that I was that important to him.

Within a few weeks, I received an invitation to a memorial service in a church on West 71st Street in New York, and I considered it an honor to have been invited. It was a very solemn service with several speakers and a minister, all of whom expressed their personal views on this man, his character as a person and his gift for drawing. But I knew that although John always received recognition, he had never made very much money. He was strictly an artist, not a businessman. The fact was, John was too kind to talk tough business language with those who negotiated with him.

A few months after John passed away, I got an invitation to a showing of his drawings at The Union League Club on East 37th Street, another esteemed venue in New York. The enclosure said:

Invitation to the Exhibition at The Union League Club

Listing of drawings/pictures in the Club with identification numbers.

I don't know how many of the drawings sold that night, but I had my eyes on the picture called

"Liberation of Paris, August 25th, 1944." This was the most outstanding picture that John ever made and to my mind, it was priceless. The size, the color, the magnitude of such direct communication of what happened that day….only someone who

POINT OF VIEW

memories of war and peace

Draw, draw, draw. Do a hundred drawings a day."

"So I did a hundred drawings a day. I sketched everything — bread lines, soup kitchens, people being evicted. This was the Depression. I copied Daumier. I copied George Grosz. I'd listen to Quin Ryan announce the White Sox games on WGN, the *Chicago Tribune* radio station — WGN stood for 'World's Greatest Newspaper.'

"As I listened, I'd imagine the action being described, and I'd draw it. I'd play records like 'Dardanella' and I'd draw what I thought the music was saying.

"In 1933 I got a break. I displayed some of my work at an art fair. One day someone left a card there. It said, 'See me, Arnold Gingrich.' So I go to the address on the card, me a barefoot kid with a beard — and he's Arnold Gingrich, a big editor about to start a new magazine called *Esquire* and, as it turns out, about to become a lifelong friend.

"Gingrich makes me his art director and he gives me 18 pages to fill — mostly with my work — for the first issue. It was dated Autumn 1933. It sold for 50 cents, a lot of money then when the *Saturday Evening Post* was a nickel. That first *Esquire* sold out its printing of 100,000 copies! I was so proud! Later, I met the art director from *College Humor*. He said, 'John Groth? You do fine work. Don't I know you from somewhere?'

"The years pass. It's World War II. The *Chicago Sun* sends me to Europe. My first story? The liberation of Paris! I'm in the first jeep to enter Paris. What joyous madness in the streets! Back at press headquarters in Normandy, I tell Bill Heinz, a great correspondent for the *New York Sun*, what I saw. He says, 'Write it.' I said I don't know how to type. He said, 'Dictate it to me. I'll type it and put

Self-portrait by John Groth

it in cables.' Which he did. We scooped the *Chicago Tribune* and I got a $2,000 bonus.

"Pretty soon I'm back in liberated Paris. I'm thinking, Picasso is here! So I look up Pablo Picasso in the phone book and find his address. I got a jeep from the motor pool and I drove to Picasso's home which is packed with people, artists, writers, poets, Andre Malraux, everybody. DeGaulle wants them to put on a program to celebrate the liberation.

"I tell Picasso's secretary I'm an American artist-war correspondent. On hearing this, Picasso asks if I'd like a private interview. Picasso's built like a six-day bicycle racer and all he's wearing is BVD shorts. I don't speak French. He doesn't speak a whole lot of English. He says, 'John Groth, you look like Joseph Conrad. I shall draw you.' I said fine but I aim to draw him, too.

"So Picasso has me climb on a bookkeeper's stool and he lies on the floor and looks up at me, his subject, which is a bit eccentric but that's Picasso. We finish our respective sketches of each other at about the same time. I gave him my sketch and then I waited for Picasso to give me his sketch of me.

"But, no. Picasso just smiled and instead gave me his dealer's card."

235

was present then could admire and appreciate this. But I could not purchase it, so I hope that some museum ended up with this fine work.

Of course, with John gone, the seasonal cards and letters no longer arrived at my door, and I realized to an even greater degree that this had been a wonderful friendship between John and me. I decided to care for and protect the artwork, together with the correspondence that had accrued over the years. I had a pretty good collection because whenever something new was about to appear in a magazine or book, John would always send me advance notice. That was how I knew to order "War Prayer," by Mark Twain, as soon as it was published.

One day, in 1991, I had an art appraiser from Hofstra University come into my home to look at some pictures that my in-laws had brought from Europe in 1937. While poking around, he spotted one of Groth's pieces. He wanted to know if I had any more because, as he said, they were of real value. I showed him my trove of drawings, and he went wild. He explained to me that this man's work was of extraordinary quality and that the drawings would surely sell at an auction that was held every week on 26th Street in Manhattan. But I did not want to part with the works, and from that day on, I realized I had to take extra good care of these drawings.

I treasured my collection of John's art, but what drove me to make some formal arrangements to preserve it was a sudden change in my health. Some time during 2001 and 2002, I fell sick and had a series of heart attacks. A stress test during 2001 revealed that the heart was damaged to the point where I needed open heart surgery.

I knew then that I would have to straighten out some financial issues and other important matters before doing anything. I would have to make some provisions for my family in case I ended up incapacitated.

While I still felt well enough to travel, I made a trip up to Harvard with my daughter because my granddaughter was accepted at their law school. I spoke to the librarian there and told her about my dossier of papers related to John Groth. I mentioned that I was willing to donate the materials to Harvard. She was quite interested in my offer and told me that Harvard had a portfolio on Groth. The items in my collection would be a welcome addition. I sensed her appeal and promised her I would follow through, which I did. I also donated correspondence with Mary Hemingway and Carlos Baker, who was a professor of English at Princeton and had written a book about Hemingway.

This donation was met with so much appreciation that I decided to take my small collection of correspondence with the late Senator Hart of Michigan and offer it to the University of Michigan, which my grandson would attend. As a

captain in the army, Hart had served with me in the Fourth Infantry Division. We were good friends and had stayed in touch through letters.

Then it was time to approach my health issues directly. I went to a most famous specialist, Dr. Richard Sholfmitz, who diagnosed the damage in detail for the cardiologist and surgeon. It was clear that balloon implants would not repair this damage, but the cardiologist played down the diagnosis and delayed any action. He said that addressing my problem would require two operations: one would be for the leg, to remove arteries that were needed for the repair, and the other was the actual repair. All this surgery, he said, was too much for me at this time. Well, I thought, if not at this time, then when? I was not going to get any younger!

Still, the doctor did not want to act immediately. But then it became clear to me that my condition was deteriorating. Within a year, and more heart attacks, I finally asked the cardiologist to please allow the operation. Even then, all he said was, "Next time you don't feel well, go to the emergency room at St. Francis Hospital."

Within a week, the operation was finally

approved. I had a recommendation for a surgeon named Dr. Taylor, who had a success record of 98 to 2. I told him I did not plan to upset his record!

The doctor asked me to see his assistant to set a date. She looked at the calendar and suggested August 6, 2002: three weeks away. The waiting period was long, but I was careful and did nothing except plan and prepare myself. I straightened out the last of the financial issues and planned to hire help for my return from the hospital.

I was admitted to the hospital on the morning of August 6th, had the surgery and by 1PM, I was in the recovery room. They let me sit for three hours, trying to avoid the pneumonia that so often follows operations in older people. How I longed to rest in my own bed! Over the next few days in the hospital, my condition improved, but I was not discharged after the usual five days. The heart needed to be observed and further stabilized. It was 10 days before they let me go home, and I could not wait to get out.

At first, I needed help night and day and I had excellent home health aides. The food was certainly better at home and the care was much more personal. I recuperated fairly quickly, receiving some visitors and sitting outdoors during the day. I was not allowed to drive for the first six weeks, and I stayed at home, resting. During this period, I was able to go through more of the documents and papers that had accumulated over the years when I was busy working and raising a family. I think perhaps it is only when nature stops us and makes us sit still that we are able to finally get to those things that have been buried for years. If we were not forced, we might otherwise not take a second look at all those papers, photos, letters and other memorabilia that sit in drawers and files.

So with this gift of time forced upon me, I was able to sort out more items that I wanted to give away. I had really precious and valuable documents from my life in the army, and by extension, from the various friends I made at that time.

In 2003, when the operation was well behind me, I began to feel stronger and ready to do important tasks again. I knew I had to retire from business and devote time to my personal affairs. One of the first undertakings was to gather all the Groth sketches that I had accrued over the years, and have them mounted uniformly and professionally.

I sorted out all these beloved drawings and looked for a good place to have them framed. I interviewed various professional framers and decided upon a special place in College Point, where the craftsmen seemed ethical and honest. The fear, rational or otherwise, was that someone might steal my treasured Groth works!

I kept this special project a secret from my children and grandchildren, as I wanted to surprise them with the results. The whole process took two weeks and the framers did a beautiful job. Now I have about 30 sketches by Groth, all signed and dated on what I call my "Museum Wall."

John Groth and I had a very special relationship, one that gives me pleasure to think about. He was a humble but great artist and an unforgettable friend.

15. REUNITING WITH OLD FRIENDS

About 10 years after my separation from the Army, I realized that there was something special to be said for having served in it, and specifically in the Fourth Infantry Division. I joined the Veterans of the Fourth Infantry Division, which was the only postwar organization in which I participated in. As a member, I enjoyed monthly meetings. There, we all met up with old friends and made new friends.

I started attending yearly reunions as well. They were held in different cities each year, and were usually arranged to cover a long weekend. Our division was called the Ivy Division, and it fulfilled my desire to be a part of a group to which I'd be proud to belong. Sometimes I'd take my wife and daughters to the events, but of course, they could not fully understand the nostalgic feelings I experienced at these reunions. Only those who live these events together can really touch their deeper meaning. For those of us who had been in the war, these meetings gave us a chance to re-live some of the tensions and hardships, to know that we were among people who knew what we had gone through.

The meetings were not mandatory. No one was forced to attend, but certainly all were welcome. A few times we were hosted by the new Fourth Division that was located in Colorado Springs. Just being there provided so much excitement: the mountains, the extraordinary scenery....I remember one event that featured a Texas-style barbecue, visits to the silver mines and other activities of local interest for tourists. Another memorable day was the one in which we rode the cog railway up Pike's Peak with the Gatlings. What a view! What a thrilling, unforgettable experience!

Back at the motel, I was introduced to the food manager, a gentleman from Würzburg. He invited me as his guest to a private dinner in the penthouse. On my way up, I grabbed my buddies, Colonel Johnson and Major Kirtly, and we settled down at a designated table, which the dining room manager had arranged for us. We felt that we were treated like kings, with a generous feast laid before us. Not a thing was missing, with all the best varieties of food and wine, surely the very finest that there was to offer. We were all most grateful for this beautiful experience.

16. IN GAUKÖNIGSHOFEN AGAIN

During the decades after the war, I made several trips back to my hometown, and each trip helped to reveal more to me about my past and the nature of my life. One journey took place in 1969, when my division made a two-week trip to Normandy Beach and other parts of Europe. I went to my village for just four hours and visited one man, a farmer, and spent some time chatting. But I soon returned to the division in Bonn. It was just a brief visit, with no overnight stay and no real emotional depth.

But then there was one trip back that I took with my grown daughter, Susan, and this was a more substantial experience. By that time, a lot of the older folks had passed away, but I found a middle-aged group, say, between 55 and 70, who had grown up under the Nazi system. In speaking with these people, it was clear to me that they were still brainwashed and held a rather distorted view of history. However, to their credit, they wanted to apologize for everything that happened and they suggested we come back and be a part of their community again.

I don't really know what it was I wanted to see or show my daughter there. We walked through the village and passed the homes that formerly belonged to Jewish people. I thought about how the former occupants had been taken away and how other people had simply appropriated their homes. Of course, my own childhood home had been sold at a fraction of its value so that my parents could get out of Germany.

I would have liked to show my daughter the house I had lived in, but it had been demolished and a school was built in its place. To say that the sterility of the new building, a perfect specimen of post WWII architecture, contrasts strongly with the charm of the house I grew up in, is an understatement.

This kind of structure, unfortunately, can be found all over Europe, and heartbreaking though it is to see such ugliness blighting the landscape, it is even more heartbreaking to think about the fate of the people who lost their homes.

I had very mixed feelings as I walked around. Certainly I felt a deep mourning for the people who were no longer there. I just could not get them out of my mind, because I knew that, in one sense, they *were* there. I knew that they had been taken away in 1942, like slaves, and none of them had returned. I knew they had almost all been exterminated. Their homes were all that was left of them. With such choked up emotions, I could not get myself to speak to any of the villagers who had taken any one of those homes. In fact, I would not be able to talk to them, even today.

But the younger group, the boys and girls today, say, from 18 - 30 whom I could speak to, they were the ones who wanted to know what really happened. The history books hadn't told them anything truthful about what took place between 1933 and 1946. That chapter was wiped out of the curriculum of German schools. These kids have not found the answers to the problem of being born German with this dreadful legacy behind them.

There was one young man, a student at the University of Bamberg and grandson of a Nazi Bürgermeister, who was so passionate about

knowing the truth that he went about writing the entire history of the Jews in Gaukönigshofen. He did meticulous research and learned that some of the Jews, who had lived in the village before the war, came from families that had been there for hundreds of years. The village had been founded in 741 and Jews had settled there in the 13th century! And so he felt compelled to write this story.

However, when he tried to ferret out the information in order to write that history, his efforts were thwarted. When it came to

Kristallnacht, all the old people in the village, including his own *mother*, clammed up and refused to speak on the topic.

He approached me and told me about the project. I was able to help him by going around to some of the old farmers I had known. Somehow, in my presence, they opened up and told the story from their perspective. The young author recorded everything that these witnesses had to say. Some even had pictures of Jewish families and offered them to him.

This started the ball rolling with the young man's book. The local mayor, who did not like the thought that this history might be published one day, forbade the author to use the names of the farmers who had kept the bonfire going all night in front of the synagogue. If the author would comply, he said, he would offer 10,000 German marks to help with the book's publication – a mere 110 copies.

After two years to research, the young man produced a 712-page book, *Die Juden in Gaukönigshofen*. The book is a masterpiece, and it resulted in the author receiving honorary Masters and Doctorate degrees from the local university.

One of the book's most poignant features is a trio of maps, which contains:

- the village itself with red spaces indicating the places where Jews once resided;
- the route to the extermination camps to the East, where the Jews were taken on March 24, 1942;
- the fate of one family, all of whose members perished on the transport.

This outstanding work provided the theme for a dedication ceremony that took place in the town hall. I was glad to attend it, and was grateful to gather even more information during the festivities.

At the ceremony, the author handed me a copy of the details from a trial that took place on November 26, 1948, and it had some very poignant words. All the accused were only identified with their initials, and their crimes read as follows:

In the name of the law, these are guilty:

Accused: H - Guilty of the crime of severe violation of safety of freedom in and disturbance of homes.

Accused: R - same as above.

Accused: P - severe violation of the law of freedom for the entire country.

Accused: H, H, B, H, and S: same as above.

This rather formal language represented the crime that these people had committed in making Jewish people feel terrorized in their own community. Primarily, the actions of which the accused were guilty reflected the principle that a citizen has the right to welfare and safety in his/her home. These accused persons had certainly violated this principle to the utmost. It was good to know that in some way, at least, justice had been served.

Part of the purpose of this visit was to dedicate the synagogue, which had been rebuilt after its destruction. Back in 1938, it had been completely and utterly ruined in the most vicious manner. But then it was restored and made into a beautiful monument. Because there are simply no Jews living in Gaukönigshofen, no one would use it as a house of worship. It is just a symbol, a holy place, a restored landmark.

My two brothers, my sister, and I were invited to

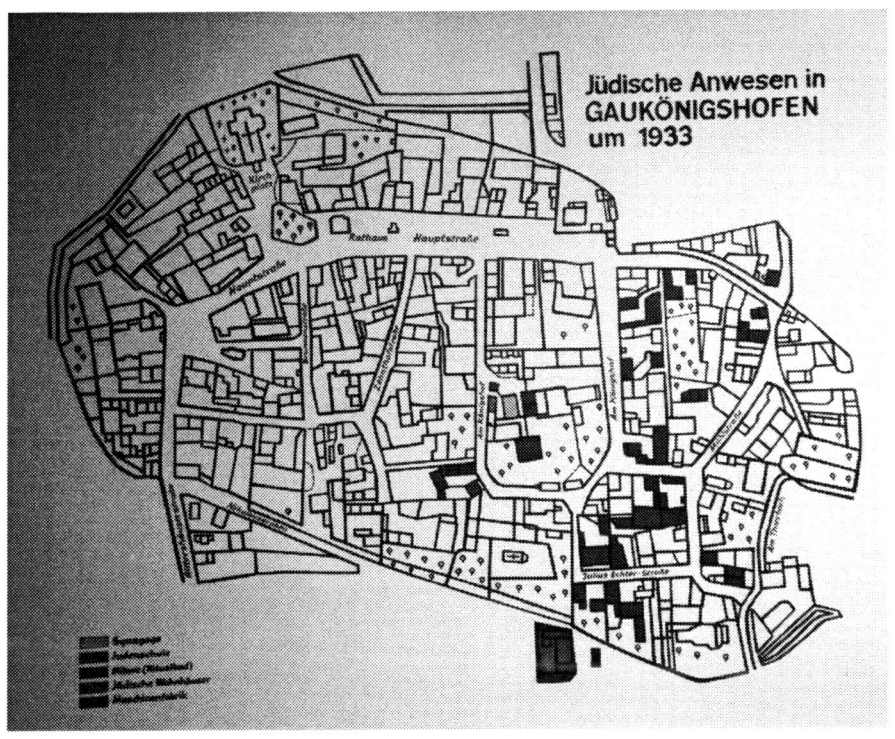

return and help dedicate the synagogue and celebrate its restoration. It was a three-day event during which I had the chance to see many of the citizens. As the townspeople congregated, there were some individuals whom I recognized and some whom I did not, since 50 years had elapsed. They had last known me as a teenager. I had grown up with them, and some of them had lived across the street from me. They seemed happy I was there. And when we did recognize each other, they'd come forward and introduce themselves.

I had wanted to make a speech at the dedication ceremony, but was not asked to. Perhaps the organizers knew it would be too heated, and did not trust me. But in the end, I was asked to say a few words.

I was prepared and determined, and once I hit the podium, I delivered my speech, in English and in German. It was sharp and honest. I told the attendees exactly what I thought and they did not like it. I told them that it was they and their brothers who had destroyed this building. It wasn't strangers. We know that, because the young author who wrote the book on the town's history researched everything and found out exactly what took place.

I wanted to tell these people that we owe it to the dead not to forget them. I wanted to remind them of what they had done on *Kristallnacht*. Some had participated in the riot, and some, equally guilty in my opinion, just stayed home and watched silently while the destruction took place. No one went outside and shouted, "Stop! Don't do this!" They did not come to the aid of one Jewish family, nor did they show any kind of courage or charity.

In fact, they did not offer any type of help at all. They just stood by silently, and I told them that I knew it.

In the crowd there was grumbling. Afterwards, some complained that I should not have said such things. Well, I thought, they did what they did, so I could say what I wanted to say! I felt that I could not just humor them when I knew that they, and maybe their fathers and grandfathers, had done such evil in their treatment or benign neglect of Jews. If given the opportunity today, I would not hesitate to repeat these words.

But of course, my thoughts were not so much with the murderers and vandals as with the people who perished during the Holocaust, the ones who never came back from exile and custody. They were ever-present in our minds and hearts. Some of them were my own friends and relatives.

After the dedication ceremony in the synagogue, one of the religious leaders from the neighboring town recited the prayer for the dead, the *Kaddish*, with all the officials standing around. There was not enough space to seat everyone. And then we, the survivors, joined together and recited this prayer. It was a very emotional experience, since we had known these victims. Why had it taken 50 years to come back and do something in their memory?

We are not just talking about a nameless, faceless population of Jews; we are talking about individuals and families, extended families, all of whom were exterminated. There is a record of each deportee because the Gestapo was so precise about recording their activities. They kept detailed, copious records of every transport that was sent away, with the name of each person, their date of birth, the date of departure, etc. All those records are printed in a book.

I sometimes wonder if the Nazis thought they would live forever because they had buried the records in a vault in a cellar, entombed in an old castle. But the American military government found the documents, and so now there are complete records of every Jew who was deported from our village. A picture of each one has been mounted in one of the rooms of the synagogue, as a memorial.

There were some other Jews present at this event, and they were very pleased with my speech.

When it was over and we all went back to the big hall for coffee and cake, I found myself surrounded by lots of people, some from the press, and some young Germans between about 16 and 20 years old. They shook hands and congratulated me on my candor and my courage to speak out as I did, and then began throwing questions at me. They asked me to come back and speak at their school. Perhaps I will do that someday because I think that the younger generation is the only future for a good Germany.

During my stay in Gaukönigshofen, I collected more stories about the horrors that had occurred there during the war. The priest told me this one: in a village a few miles away, a British plane was either shot down or had made an emergency landing. Four people came out alive: the pilot, the co-pilot and the crew. But the local S.A. director from the village killed those four soldiers, single handedly, with a pitchfork.

The priest had them buried in the Jewish cemetery. Eventually, though, these bodies were moved, because they belonged to the allied forces. There is an old Jewish cemetery about five miles away from the village. It had been part of ten communities. And that, amazingly, was not touched! I learned that it remained unscathed because, as the local village priest told me, "Mr. Kleeman, I preached every Sunday morning that anyone who commits a crime against the dead people will be punished." That's the only reason the cemetery was kept in good shape. There was not one stone thrown over or damaged. No, only the living were destroyed.

For me, the trip back was hard, but it was still worthwhile. There were a couple of fellows who had been asked to participate but refused because their parents had been taken away and had not survived. They were not lucky, as I was, to be able to take my parents out of Germany alive. For some reason, God had spared us and had been good to us. How could I ever fathom why I had had the privilege of saving my entire immediate family? Because of this I felt it was an honor and a duty to go to this event. And when it was all over, I could think back on these 50 years and what they have meant in my life.

17. RETURNING TO LUXEMBOURG

In 1994, the American army organized a celebration for the 50th anniversary of D-Day, which was to take place on June 6th, in Normandy. I went with my old war buddy, Major Fiset, who was then 82 years old. We met at the Frankfurt airport and planned to drive to Normandy together, hoping to make a meaningful and sentimental journey out of it. We had been looking forward to this special day, one in which we would take time to remember the friends we had lost a half century before.

I will digress from the travelogue to say that my relationship with Lewis Fiset is a rich one, and particularly significant because at the time of this writing, he is one of the few war buddies who is still alive.

He entered the service in 1940 and graduated at the top of the officers' class. His was the first class to be completed after the war was declared.

It was not long before Fiset's fine character came to the attention of General Barton, who brought him into the 4th Infantry Division.

When he first came into the army, Fiset was assigned post of Barton's Junior Aide, a responsible position for which he was well qualified. One had to be a model of trust, discretion, excellent behavior and judgment to be selected for this role.

Fiset was sent with the advance group to England to choose a venue for the Division headquarters. This was quite a responsibility, one that he would execute in an exemplary manner.

After about eight months on the job, Fiset came to the Military Government office as a special agent. I was the interpreter in the section, and it was there that we were introduced.

We immediately hit it off. When he learned that I was Jewish, he confided in me that his very first job ever had been as a "Shabbos Goy." He was in the service of religious Jewish people, turning their lights on and off for them during Shabbos, and keeping their fires going, since these two tasks are considered to be "work," which is forbidden for the 24 hours of Shabbos.

The Senior Aide was Captain Philip Hart, a smart lawyer from Michigan. (Fiset would eventually be promoted to this senior position.) Both men being Catholic, they immediately got on together and jokingly called me the "Jew Boy." Nowadays, such a moniker sounds derogatory, but at the time, it was merely affectionate. Terms such as these change in value as society evolves.

Fiset and I were assigned to the Military Government Section in Paris, where I was given the task to driving the Major around on his special missions. One of these was to work with a Professor Burleth, who was going to help us get around Paris. For three days, we picked him up early in the morning at his apartment in the Neuilly section of Paris, and he would spend the day with us. Late at night we would drive him home through the city that was cloaked in darkness. This is no mean feat when one thinks about Paris with its maze of diagonal and one-way streets, which are confusing even in the light of day.

When it was time to leave Paris, we headed to Belgium, and the professor stayed behind. Belgium presented a new set of experiences for us, for as we arrived and posted the proclamations for the local people, many an American Air Corps officer came up to greet us. These officers turned out to be pilots who had been shot down or pulled out of burning planes.

They were dressed in local style clothing because they had been in hiding, and so were meant to blend in with the population. Charitable people had taken them in and frequently provided quarters for them in hidden rooms. The host would install a "dummy wall" and would move an armoire in front of it so that when Germans came to search the house, the officer would not be discovered.

There was not much we could do for these pilots, but we did instruct them to wait another day or two, in which time we would arrange for them to be picked up. In our time there, we must have encountered about 75 of these pilots!

In December, 1944, Fiset and I were in Luxembourg. The German army broke through the American lines then, causing lots of damage and creating panic. We were not far from the front and the danger of being captured was acute. One night, we settled in an old farm house that comprised a barn for the animals and living quarters for the family. We secured our jeep in the barn and bedded down for the night. Fiset made me sleep in the room with him, which was against Army regulations, but he insisted. I could only surmise that this arrangement made him feel more secure.

Fiset was promoted to the rank of Major in March of 1945. His progress through the ranks was not undeserved, for he was an exemplary soldier. Whenever possible, we traveled together and always got on very well. We had a kind of mutual respect and never quarreled. And so it made perfect sense that 50 years later, we would be traveling together again, this time for an important anniversary.

We had been looking forward to this excursion. There were going to be speeches and commemorative ceremonies and we assumed it would be a worthwhile endeavor.

Our journey began with our heading out of Frankfurt and going toward Bleialf, the village we had evacuated back in 1944, and the one in which we had met John Groth and Ernest Hemingway. We were hoping to meet with the mayor there, but at the time of our arrival he was not around. Too bad, because we had so many questions to ask him about what had happened to the village since the war.

That night, we slept at the Gasthof Zwicker, another nostalgic spot, where we had eaten lunch back in '44. The new owners knew nothing about the last 50 years' worth of history in Bleialf, or at least they were not saying....

Then we continued on to Luxembourg. En route, we stopped in at the Villa Vauban, where we had lived for two weeks, in December of '44 when we were in charge of the military government. The Villa Vauban must be one of the most elegant buildings in Luxembourg. It is complete with stables, a swimming pool, a music room, and all the other amenities of what we think of as "Old World" European luxury.

When we stood at the gates of the villa, military personnel came to question us, asking why we wanted to go in. We told them of our history and experience there, hoping we'd get them to admit us for a look around, for old times' sake. After long deliberations, they told us, "This is now the home of the Kronprinz, and you cannot go in."

Evidently, since the prince was not in town, we were not allowed in the chateau. We reflected that back in 1944, he had not been there to stop us then from moving in! (Later, though the prince himself sent an apology for not having been there to receive us.)

We remembered that back in 1944 the Battle of the Bulge started, so the stay was not so pleasant. The Germans were in force about 20 miles away and their plans were to re-take the City of Luxembourg.

At that time, a Lieutenant Bailey was transferred to the 106th Division. The division had arrived from the States and took over the Bleialf area that we had occupied. The main thrust of the Battle of the Bulge was the Bleialf area, and the 106th Division lost two regiments; they had been captured by the German surprise attack. Poor Lieutenant Bailey was caught there, but being a true outdoorsman, he went into hiding and wandered, during the night, toward the American lines. After three days, he made his way back to us in Luxembourg and then returned to the 106th. This was a life and death march for him, but he survived it! I am reminded of him because among my memorabilia is my original pass, signed by

Luxembourg

Bailey, allowing me to visit the City of Luxembourg after duty hours.

Lieutenant Bailey played a role in my life later on, too. Some time after the war I traveled through Raleigh and stopped at his law office and he took me home for dinner that night. We spent some time reminiscing about our days in Europe.

Bailey went on to become a judge, and we kept in touch. Some years later, my daughter Susan got married, and Judge Bailey, ever the sportsman, attended the wedding, arriving in his own plane!

All of these memories came back as a result of this journey back into my past......

*   *   *   *   *   *   *   *

After our stay in Luxembourg, Major Fiset and I continued on to Normandy, for what was supposed to be the main feature and focus of the trip. But the actual celebration turned out to be a disappointment, largely because of the way the French handled it. They mounted a rather festive event which they called a "Golden Jubilee," a name and a mood so unfitting for what should have been a solemn occasion. And so before the first speech was even delivered, Major Fiset and I packed up and left, heading nonstop for Switzerland. We could not get away fast enough and sped out of there, driving 10 hours to Bad Zurzach, where we spent one week before returning home.

My friendship with Lewis Fiset continues to this day. He has lived for a long time in San Antonio, Texas, and 30 years ago, I paid him a visit.

He never married. He had been badly wounded in 1945 near Bad Mergentheim, Germany, and spent two years in the hospital. As a result, he had to learn to walk all over again.

> **PASS**
>
> Tec 5   Werner Kleeman   32494091
> (Rank)   (Name)   (ASN)
>
> has permission to be absent from his place of duty between the hours of 1700 and 2300 to visit the city of Luxembourg.
>
> OFFICIAL
> Allied Expeditionary Force
> Military Government
>
> JAMES H. POU BAILEY,
> 1st Lieutenant, FA,
> Deputy Civ Affairs O
>
> Military Government Officer

He started studying for the priesthood, a dream that had been deferred years ago. Alas, this was not to be. His legs were sufficiently damaged such that he could not tolerate long periods of standing, which is certainly part of a priest's vocation.

Today, he lives in a lovely house with, as I remember, a fig tree out front. He made a peaceful life for himself there in Texas.

Visiting him was a wonderful experience. We strolled along San Antonio's beautiful River Walk and spoke of times gone by. I spent the night in a room with about 80 statues of the Madonna – this was Fiset's collection – and I like to think they watched over me as I slept.

Lewis Fiset is a wonderful man, a kind, inspiring human being, humble and decent as well. He is now 93, and I am 87, and we can still enjoy picking up the phone and hearing each other's voices. Friendships that were made on the battle fields have a special bond that cannot really be described with words. One must live this in order to appreciate its value.

18. ENDURING AND CONTROVERSIAL RELATIONSHIPS

My much respected friend, Major Gatling, also reappeared in my life. In 1948, with some war years behind me, I set out to find him. I was in the process of buying my home in Queens, where I would eventually raise my family. Knowing that Gatling was in Westchester, I looked him up in the local telephone directory.

It was at his Wall Street office, where he was a corporate real estate lawyer, that I finally located him. The house-buying project is what brought us together again.

Once I was settled in my new home, I would call Gatling from time to time. He used to invite me to visit him and have lunch at his downtown office and we established a semi-annual visiting routine. Once in awhile I'd go to his home for Sunday afternoon dinner. This became a regular tradition for many years, and I always felt welcome.

Gatling was obviously not afraid of change, because in the time I knew him, he lived in a variety of places. He had a large house in Pleasantville, then moved to a small apartment there. Subsequently, he and his wife bought a large house in Mount Kisco, and then moved again, this time to an apartment in Somers, New York. Finally, Gatling went to a retirement apartment in Connecticut, knowing that it had a nursing home attached to it for people who might need extra help. Eventually, this was the final place where Colonel Gatling would live until the end of his life.

When he died, at the age of 83, I attended a memorial service for him with some members of the Fourth Division and 12th Infantry Regiment. The ashes were buried in the Gatling family plot in Virginia. Later, when Mrs. Gatling passed on, I attended that service for her. I felt that I owed this to the family, as they had treated me like a son.

I have only happy memories of our visits. Gatling had been such a gracious host, making it easy for us to discuss old experiences from the war, relaxing over a cocktail, some cheese and our reminiscences. Because I had become a special part of the family, I learned of their travails as well as their good fortune.

The Gatlings had two children. When their daughter, Melissa, who was born about seven years before the war, started college, she it seemed to me that she suddenly became a problem to her parents. A bright girl, she was in school in Virginia, majoring in Russian. For no reason that was apparent to me, there was suddenly a gulf between her and her mother. There was no obvious justification that I could see; she just appeared to be estranged from her mother, and by extension from both parents.

After completing college, Melissa went to London to continue studying. While there, she fell in love with a Ceylonese man, who was also studying in London. Being rather bright, he loved learning and was a kind of perpetual student.

I felt that this brought Melissa a measure of unhappiness later on, because once she was married, she had to work to support him. I knew Melissa to be an educated woman, and learned that she had to be as resourceful as possible, doing work that was beneath her intellectual capacity, as one often does in order to keep life going.

During those years, the Melissa's mother told me that her daughter did not communicate with her. Occasionally, her father would get a letter from her at his office. Then Melissa's husband took her on a trip to Ceylon, the two of them driving there from Europe in a jeep! She never spoke much about this but I can only imagine that it was a wild and somewhat fantastic experience for a girl who came from such a cultivated, conservative family.

Eventually the couple returned to England, and shortly afterwards, Melissa gave birth to two boys. In 1969, I happened to be in England for the Fourth Division's 25th anniversary, and I contacted Melissa and invited her for dinner. I also invited a Colonel Johnson, who had been a comrade of Melissa's father in the 12th Infantry Regiment.

At dinner, Melissa did not tell us anything about her marriage or of her lifestyle, but I could see her rough, hardworking hands; I took this to be a telltale sign of manual labor. It seemed like a difficult package: a husband, two children and hard work.

A few years later, Melissa got divorced and, after

many years of separation, came home to live with her parents. They bought the large house in Mount Kisco, which had a private apartment that Melissa moved into, so the boys went to the school there. Ultimately, though, Melissa ended up in Florida, and I knew little of her for a while after that.

The Gatlings also had a son, Kent. He had been sent away to Wisconsin to attend a boarding school that was run by an army friend. Kent was a devoted student, and with some help, he got a good education and later became a school teacher. Eventually, he achieved the rank of principal at a school in Bennington, Vermont.

Once, on my way to New Hampshire, I stopped by to see him and spent the night there. He had bought himself a large, old home, situated on spacious grounds in the center of town. By this time, he and his wife, a farm girl from Connecticut, had two children, who were now in college.

After both parents passed away, Kent broke up the Gatlings' apartment. As a memento, he gave me a beautiful end table, which still graces my living room.

More than a decade after Major Gatling died, I made a wonderful discovery. The little end table had been sitting in my living room, but unbeknownst to me, it had a compartment that contained a true treasure. One day, when I moved the table, I lifted the lid. Inside was a small paperbound book, its cover yellowed with age. The title, printed in red, read *Les Pommiers ont Refleuri* (The Apple Trees are in Bloom Again). It was a book of poetry, written in French, and the author was Simone Renaud, the wife of the erstwhile Mayor of Ste. Mère Eglise!

I flipped though the small volume and saw that it had been published in 1951. On the title page was a lovely handwritten inscription:

Un fidèle et affectueux Hommage à Major Gatling Jr. (A faithful and affectionate homage to Major Gatling, Jr.) *A Hero from the IVth Infantry Division (Ivy) who fought victoriously to liberate Sainte-Mère-Eglise in 1944. Simone Renaud, who will never forget.*

Fortunately, some of these poems were translated into English, and it was very touching to read them. While all literature is better in the original language, one can still appreciate the poet's sweet sentiments, albeit in translation.

The poems all deal with the same theme – the author's honor and gratitude to those who helped preserve the sanctity of France. Throughout the book are also some simple, delicate ink drawings done by the author's son.

Finding this book in my own house, where it was hidden for so many years, was a most delightful surprise. I cannot help but wonder if Colonel Gatling's children simply did not know that it was in that compartment of the table. At any rate, I feel it has found the right home, here with me, and I cherish it as a part of my collection of wartime mementoes.

I stayed in touch with Gatling's children. When I celebrated my 80th birthday in 1999, I invited Kent and his wife to the party and they came down from Vermont. To me, this was a great honor, and I was happy to see them. It brought back memories and we now exchange cards at Christmastime. I also hear from Melissa from time to time, and it is an honor to still be in touch with these people.

*　　*　　*　　*　　*　　*　　*　　*

By contrast, there was the story of Colonel Stone, whom I never liked and did not respect, despite

> *En fidèle et affectueux*
> *Hommage*   Dédié à mes Fils.
> *à Major N. P. Gatling Jr.*
> *a Hero from IVth Infantry Division (Ivy)*
> *who fought victoriously to liberate*
> *Sainte-Mère-Eglise in 1944*
>
> **" LES POMMIERS ONT REFLEURI "**
> *(Appletrees are in bloom again)*
>
> *Simone Renaud*
>
> *who will never forget...*

the fact that we had been in the service together. But although I did not admire Stone, there was still valuable experience to be gleaned from having known him.

Apart from my own experience with the Colonel, there were things I learned about him that made me feel that, in a sense, he had brought about the death of his own son. Stone was frustrated that he

Traduction anglaise du poème précédent.

Dedicated to the American Mothers.

THE GREAT CEMETERIES UNDER THE SNOW

(Military American Cemeteries of Sainte-Mère-Eglise : number 1 and number 2)

The snow, this night
Has fallen softly from the clouds
To spread its marvelous mantle
On the wooden crosses.

Nature, for once, has made herself
Merciful and maternal for the poor dead,
By gently weaving thousands of flowers
And thousands of wings (feathers)
In order their shroud might be more soft.

Feathers of swans, flowers from heavenly gardens,
A net as light as air
Laid on their last wound and their last gesture,
Like a breath and a kiss...

Whether it be the newly born,
Or the pure forehead of the Virgin
Or the silver chalice so bright on the altar,

had never been promoted to the rank of general, and so he wanted his son to become the general in the family. He sent him to a series of private schools, then a prep school that prepared him for West Point. The son was accepted there, and attended. After graduating from West point, the young man signed up for helicopter training in Alabama.

Stone and his wife moved to Brielle, New Jersey, and when their son came home on leave, he took out a helicopter from the military base in Lakehurst and flew over Brielle to wave to his parents. This was a lighthearted activity, but after that, he was sent to war in Southeast Asia, and flying over Vietnam was different from flying over Brielle.

Then one day, Colonel Gatling and I read in *The New York Times* that the promising young man had been shot down. Gatling and I called each other and waited to hear more. Then a call came from Colonel Stone, informing us that his son was dead and that the funeral would take place at West Point.

We drove to the service at the chapel. We both felt the obligation to go there, although we really did not like Colonel Stone. In fact, our dislike for him was so strong that we could not bring ourselves to attend the reception at the Officers' Club. We simply drove back to Manhattan.

About one or two months later we decided, again out of obligation, to pay a visit to the Colonel in New Jersey. We found him sitting in his recliner in the living room. An American flag was installed next to the chair on a pole. On one side of the room was a table upon which lay a binder. It contained all the letters that Stone had sent home to his wife from his own days during the Second World War. I remembered then that he had written his wife a letter every day at 5PM. Back on the home front, Mrs. Stone had typed them out and put them in a folder. I would have loved to have read some of them, just to see what he had reported about our life at war, but I did not ask to see them. On the very same table was the flag that had covered Stone's son's casket. The flag had been folded military style at the funeral. The table, then, was a kind of small shrine, a place of memory and contemplation about the events of two wars.

Gatling and I only stayed for about 20 minutes.

The Colonel asked us if we wanted a Scotch, plain or with soda. That was the visit! As soon as we got on the road I told Gatling that I needed to stop for a cup of coffee. He agreed.

Over our coffee, we discussed the visit and agreed that we both felt as though we had been sitting at a court martial, being accused of something. There was no warmth from Stone and similarly, none from us. We had only made the visit out of duty. Not all relationships yield the same richness of experience, but there is always something one can learn, even if it is about oneself.

*   *   *   *   *   *   *   *

Freddie Strauss comes up again and again in my life's story.... Long after the war, when Freddie had settled and established a business in Syracuse, NY, I went up to see him and spent a weekend there. By this time, he had three sons, ages two, four and six. I already knew Freddie's wife Betty, whom I had met in Chicago years ago in my post-Army days, while looking for work.

Shortly after my visit, Freddie passed away and was buried in New York, where the Strauss family had its own plot. I attended the funeral, which was a sad occasion, especially since Freddie, throughout the years, had played various pivotal roles in my life. I kept in touch with Betty and when she remarried a few years later, I was happy to still be included as a family friend.

Then about five years ago, I got a call from Freddie's youngest son, Robert, who was by this time grown man of 45. He was planning a trip to Germany to uncover the roots of his father, grandmother and stepfather. Betty had told him that I would be the ideal man to help with this project, and of course, I was glad to be enlisted.

I knew that the grandmother's village was Wiesenbronn, one that might not be too well known to an outside visitor. I sent Robert maps of the area and advised him as to the best route there from France, which was to be his point of entry.

He did make the trip with his wife and daughter, and in spite of the fact that he did not speak German, was able to find not only the village, but also the cemetery where his ancestors were buried. It was a successful journey and he accomplished his mission.

Upon his return, I met with him and he told me

everything about the trip. Subsequently, he wrote a newspaper article about the adventure.

This curious young man went on to become the Director of the Peace Corps in Cameroon, and as I write, has now completed five years of work there. It would have been nice for Freddie to see his son in such a successful and meaningful role in the world.

*　　*　　*　　*　　*　　*　　*　　*

In this memoir, I have only briefly mentioned my good friend, J.D. Salinger. Jerry, as many people know, is an intensely private person who, despite his great fame, wanted as little said about him as possible. I will respect that wish by paying him tribute, but also by keeping it brief and war-related.

In one of the many letters I have, documenting my decades-long relationship with Jerry, he refers to an event that took place during WWII. The letter is dated 1961, and he writes from his home in Vermont. Of course, much had transpired since our days in Europe, and Jerry is responding to some of my references to those days:

RFD 2 - Windsor, Vermont - September 5, 1961

Dear Werner,

Forgive this delayed reply. We've had a roughish summer up here, for complicated reasons that I'll tell you about one day if we ever have that blow-out in town. Anyway, it's fine to hear from you. And the news about John is good, too. As I write this, incidentally, a letter just came through from Jack Altaras. He has a law practice in Texas, and has a son going into high school this year. And so we're all middle aged geezers. No secret, I guess.

That's interesting about Israel, I wonder, too if you've ever visited your brother there. The whole country should be wonderfully worth seeing.

I have the feeling you must have been saddened, too, over the fact and circumstance of Hemingway's death. Remember the little house where we were staying during the Huertgen Forest business? I remember his kindness, and I'm sure you do, too.

My little girl, Peggy, starts school this fall. We'll still have one at home, though, an Eskimo Husky pup.

I still haven't been to N.Y., Werner, in heaven knows when, but one of these months or years I'll make it, and when I do, we'll have a big fat lunch or dinner together, I hope. It will be great to see you.

Yours ever,
Jerry

When Salinger says "I remember his kindness and I am sure you do, too," he is referring to one dreary evening at around 8PM, when we were both staying in the same house in Zweifall. He suddenly said to me, "Let's go and look up Hemingway." With that, we put on our coats, took a flashlight and started walking. After about a mile, we found a small brick house and noticed a marker P.R.O., which meant "Public Relations Office." A few steps up we found a side doorway, which we entered.

Inside we found Captain Stevenson, who was in charge of the office, and there was Hemingway, stretched out on a couch. A visor on his forehead, he was busy writing on a yellow pad. The office had its own generator to produce electricity for war reporters who had checked in for the night. The rest of the town lay in blackness.

I felt elated to have the chance to visit once again one of the world's giants, the author who had recently finished *For Whom the Bell Tolls*. I had met up with him about two months before in Bleialf, when I was able to inquire about the two beautiful women whom he loved and admired, Marlene Dietrich and Ingrid Bergman. And now, here I was, sitting with Giant and the young aspiring author, Salinger, who had already published several stories. While we sipped champagne from aluminum cups, I was fascinated, thinking that I was in the presence of such gifted men and was able to observe them in such a natural setting. And when I received Jerry's letter 17 years later, I thought about how yes, I did remember that evening just as if it were yesterday. Something so unusual and eventful stays in one's mind for a lifetime. There, in the midst of my official duty, was this unique experience.

I was always so proud to know Salinger, especially since I knew him before he was famous. Many years later, his books became *de riguer* for high school English students. I wanted my granddaughter Allison to see how prolific a writer he had become. We visited one of the newly erected Barnes and Noble stores, which were a novelty at the time. Never before had there been a bookstore of such magnitude, in which one could sit in a plush armchair and peruse the books of one's choice. The smell of freshly-brewed coffee wafts through the store, creating a cozy atmosphere conducive to exploring books.

I took Allison over to the "Salinger shelf," and there we found all of his works displayed. I was so pleased to see a label with his name on it. Certainly, this is the minimum that he deserves!

*   *   *   *   *   *   *   *

In my account of my war, days, I did not pay tribute to Colonel Russell P. Reeder, but I shall do so now. This honorable man took me under his wing after he returned home from the war, where he was wounded after only five days in Normandy. The shell damage to his leg was so severe that at Walter Reade Army Hospital the doctors had to amputate. Reeder never complained about this and after 19 months in and out of the hospital, he went to work at West Point as the Athletic Director, since he was a sportsman as well as a soldier.

He was hospitalized at a veteran's hospital in upstate New York, near Hopewell, when I paid him a visit. I had just returned from Israel, and so I brought Reeder a gift: it was a rock that came from King Solomon's mines, near Elat (at least that was the story my brother told me). This rock became a valuable piece of history in the Reeder home. I was told that every visitor who came to the house was compelled to handle it, to smell it, to hold it next to their ear to hear its "sounds." People just fell in love with this keepsake!

After that, I used to visit Reeder near West Point. Then, when he moved to Virginia, I saw him at his new assisted living facility. I remember sharing a lovely dinner with him in the facility's dining room. We were both aware of our very special relationship.

Reeder wrote books and I was invited to say something about him for the cover of the last one. I am still terribly in awe of this honor, I - an enlisted man, and foreign born, to be asked to play a role in this man's life.

When I became inspired to write a book about my own life, it was Reeder who created a "blueprint" for me, advising me as to what I should include and in what order. He asked me to write a note for the new book he was publishing, "Born at Reveille," an invitation that touched me deeply.

As a final honor, I was invited to attend the funerals of Colonel Reeder and his wife, both of which were held at West Point.

*　　*　　*　　*　　*　　*　　*　　*

It is certainly hard to tell the events of one's life in the order in which they occurred, since memory does not follow any sequence. All events seem to be intertwined, one giving rise to the other, the layers melding together.

Much of what is in the text of this book regarding *Kristallnacht* is taken from a conversation I had back in 1988 with anchorman Garrick Uttley. At that time, I was asked to participate in a segment on NBC's Today Show, in which I spoke about that dreadful event and gave a firsthand, eyewitness account. It was the 50th anniversary of the tragedy, and an apt time to have television audiences learn more about it.

The segment consisted of an interview with some very pointed questions, most of which I had to consider strongly before answering. Again, memories do not necessarily come back in order. They rise up when the question is posed.

Kristallnacht is an extremely painful topic for anyone who lived through it, but it is valuable for people to learn about while its victims are still alive. The photo shows Mr. Uttley as he is interviewing me, and a bit of the flier announcing the broadcast.

National Broadcasting 30 Rockefeller Plaza
Company, Inc. New York, NY 10112
212 664-4444

 October 28, 1988

Werner Kleeman will appear in a segment dealing with Kristallnacht on the Sunday Today Show airing November 13, 1988. In New York the show is broadcast from 9am to 10:30am.

19. MY EIGHTIETH BIRTHDAY

In 1999, when I was turning 80, my wonderful daughters made plans to throw a gala party for me, which many of my favorite people would attend. It was supposed to be a surprise, but it was not long before their plan was revealed. Just as well, as I was able to participate in creating the guest list.

Not only was this party a great success, but it was a meaningful gathering that will always be absolutely unforgettable. The 40-person guest list included family, friends, business associates, military buddies and assorted other dear acquaintances from various parts of my long life.

We celebrated at an intimate French restaurant on Long Island, where the owner, who is also the chef, went to his usual high standard of great pains to produce lovely food and make everyone feel the warmth and festive atmosphere.

Perhaps most meaningful of all for me, though, was that Kent, the son of my beloved friend, Colonel Gatling, came in down from Vermont. Just thinking of this brings tears to my eyes.

Roberta Oster, who was responsible for making such a difference in my life, was unable to not attend, as she was on her honeymoon in Asia. She did, however, send a monumental piece of writing, in my honor:

A Birthday Note for Werner Kleeman from Roberta Oster Sachs

Werner Kleeman might be turning 80 – but to those of us who know him – he's always going to be a young man. A man with a sparkle in his eye, a love of his family and a zest for life. He is an inspiration to all who meet him – and I am honored to share this memory with you…and to return to you what Werner gave to me…his legacy…in his own words.

Werner Kleeman changed my life. I was 23-year old researcher at NBC News and was sent to a World War II veterans' reunion in Pennsylvania to find men for Tom Brokaw to interview for our "D-Day" 40th anniversary broadcast. The criteria were tough: the veterans had to have landed on D-Day at exactly "H" hour, they had to have vivid memories of that moment and be able to tell their stories with passion. I spoke with over forty men during the weekend who all had incredible stories…but no one had a story like Werner's – and when he opened up his heart – he brought a wealth of wisdom and taught me, and millions of Americans, about courage and honor.

I remember when Werner stopped me and said, "My name is Werner Kleeman, and I am a proud Fourth Division veteran and I landed on D-Day at H-hour and I want to tell you my story." When I heard his German accent and saw the pain in his eyes, I knew this was something important. Werner told me how Nazi soldiers in his small German town of

Gaukönigshofen came to his front door, arrested him and his father, and sent Werner to Dachau. He told me of how he got out of Dachau by getting a letter from a relative in England who was willing to sponsor him, and then sent for the rest of the family, saving most of them from the death camps. Werner then came to America and was drafted into the Fourth Division.

Werner spoke about working side by side with Ernest Hemingway and J.D. Salinger, and a man named Hart who later became a US Senator. Miraculously, Werner survived the D-Day landing and made it through France to Germany. He ultimately became the first US soldier to liberate his hometown in Germany and arrest the very officer who had sent his family, and so many other Jews, to die in the gas chambers. And every step along the way, Werner told his story with dignity and pride.

NBC ultimately filmed Werner's incredible story – in Normandy, France, and Tom Brokaw interviewed him on the beach-head where he landed as a young soldier. Werner's daughter Susan came along for the trip and I remember sitting in a small restaurant in St. Mère Eglise with her at the moment she realized why NBC was so impressed with her father. For over 30 years Werner had not told Susan nor Deborah of his Dachau *days. He kept this all to himself until he could no longer hold it back – and when Susan realized what was happening, her eyes filled with tears. I know that she was glad that he was finally able to share his past, and she understood why it took him so long, and why he had protected her and her sister.*

After the broadcast ran on NBC on June 6th, 1984, Werner spoke out even more about his story and even agreed to go back to his hometown of Gaukönigshofen and help the local authorities identify Jewish graves, the old synagogue, and the few relics left of the Jewish community there. He gave interviews to German newspapers and entertained pitches from Hollywood producers to tell his story.

Werner also agreed to spend time with me to tell his life story on tape for a biography, so we began taping interviews. Now you will have this legacy. I have copied the transcripts for Werner's children and grandchildren. They will learn the story of a courageous man who helped so many people and who continues to be the greatest father…and friend…and inspiration.

I am sorry I cannot be with you on this day – I will be on my honeymoon in China and India, but my heart is with you – all of the Kleeman family and friends, and especially with Werner, who has brought so much to all the people whose lives he has touched. I look forward to celebrating his 85th, and 95th and 105th birthdays ...and to more and more stories to keep all of us inspired and...on our toes.

With much love,

Roberta Oster Sachs

I suppose I should have made a speech, but all I could manage was a few words. I was so overcome with the turnout and the utter joy of being surrounded by so many wonderful people.

Mr. Munzel, the German consul, was there (he was actually the Second Consul at the time, and is now stationed in Houston as the First Consul) He comes from Karlstadt, a little German town near to where my mother was born. Because of this, I feel a certain kinship with him and his wife.

All my siblings were there, including my brother who lives in Israel. The photo shows us, left to right: Siggy, Theo (now deceased), myself, Alfred and Ruth.

There were other important friends and

acquaintances who could not be present, such as Theodore Roosevelt IV. He did, however, send an affectionate note.

My daughter Debby wrote a little vignette, which she read aloud. She wanted to address so many points, and was filled with so much love, that she condensed her thoughts into this piece of writing. As I re-read it, I see a mixture of tenderness, appreciation, pride and admiration. What more could one ask for from a daughter. To be loved that way is without measure.

Sept. 26, 1999

Dear Dad:

When I think about my father, I think about his great love for my sister and I. He has raised us to be independent people, to lean on ourselves and to be self-motivated. Whatever we accomplish, he is always proud of us.

This week I watched Saving Private Ryan for the first time. My father landed on Utah Beach in Normandy. What he experienced lives on in his heart. He never related the details or the anguish to me. I am in awe of my own father, of what he's accomplished to make history as we know it, to save lives, to be able to continue on.

I think he's an amazing person. Today he is 80. A day doesn't go by that he doesn't educate himself, whether it be by reading the newspaper, or having daily discussions with Ruth over the stock market, or by seeking answers to questions relating to business.

He has taken me under his wing, so to speak, to teach me to take over his business. And I've come to realize that no one person can stand in his shoes. Without exaggeration, four people could not handle what he accomplishes on a daily basis. And, no one has his remarkable salesmanship, personality, sincerity, or expertise.

LEHMAN BROTHERS

THEODORE ROOSEVELT IV
MANAGING DIRECTOR

August 25, 1999

Mr. Werner Kleeman
45-46-196th Place .
Flushing, New York 11358-3530

Dear Werner:

    I was both delighted and dismayed to learn that you will be celebrating your 80th Birthday shortly. Eighty is certainly worth celebrating but dismayed that I will not be able to attend and to congratulate you in person. I cannot tell you how much I enjoyed talking with you and exchanging correspondence over World War 11 over the last year. You were certainly as good an example as any that Tom Brokaw talks about in his book, *The Forgotten Generation.* Your willingness to pick up arms and do the right thing and then rebuild the nation following World War 11 is a legacy all future generations should remember in honor.

    Happy Birthday, and I hope to see you in the relatively near future.

Sincerely yours,

Theodore Roosevelt IV

I've been told by Hannah that he has "old world charm" and it is rare and wonderful, but that isn't for me to talk about.

Dad, I would like to use words you've spoken to us. "Every day of your life you do honor to yourself and all of our family."

Our thoughts are with you.
Our thanks are with you.
Our love is with you.
Our prayers are for you.
I hope you know, we will always be here for you.

With love always,

Debby, Lee, Laura and Steven

Of course, I received no less affection from my other daughter and of course my four grandchildren, all of whom I am very proud. It is indeed a privilege to see one's 80th year, to be alive and healthy and surrounded by so many precious souls.

20. LIFE AS IT IS TODAY

I have been thinking about some of my observations on life and have asked myself what has left the greatest impression on me during the last 80 years? I have a few answers to my own question.....

To have been able to live through and participate in D-Day, to have gone through the training for that event, and to prepare mentally and physically for it, was extraordinary. It was evolutionary to have helped in the defeat of Germany, to destroy

the Nazi regime. I did my part to try and teach some old and young Germans that the freedom they won must be utilized to start a new democracy within their borders and to rebuild their nation. This took years and, with the help of the Marshall Plan, it appears that they succeeded. A nation that was once our enemy is now our ally and has become a world power again.

To live through a darkness and watch a quiet and calm revolution inside of Russia change its political system from Bolshevism to democracy under the leadership of Michael Gorbachov... this transfiguration occurred without a single shot being fired or any one person being executed. It is a miracle that this could happen the way it did, in modern times.

Thinking about these sociopolitical changes leads me to reflect not only upon what happened in Germany, but has happened and can happen in other countries. Just as America joined the allies in the war against Germany, Japan joined with Germany in its plan to rule the world. It took a few years to build the war machine and prepare the world for the restoration of peace, freedom and normality. Slowly, this happened and the tide turned. After the war ended in Europe, the power was moved to the other theatre in order to defeat Japan. They too, had conquered various parts of the world, places they had no right to attack and occupy.

When the U.S. dropped atomic bombs on Hiroshima and Nagasaki, Japan was forced to surrender and realize that their false dream would not be tolerated in the world. And they too became a world power again, through hard work. Today they are enjoying this achievement. In the meantime, China has joined the free world and is another power that will be accepted.

But the Arab world, as I write this, does not seem ready to live in peace and enjoy the freedom to live life to the utmost. It is still part of a world that practices murder and killing to achieve their goals. There is hatred among the people, so one can never feel safe within its boundaries. The Jews have liberated and occupied their own land after thousands of years in the Diaspora and have great problems protecting themselves and living peacefully within these borders. We do not know if or when there will be peace, and it is not foreseeable now.

During my lifetime, we have conquered the world in the scientific field. Humankind has traveled to the moon and come back with samples of rock. Even God did not tell us this might happen in our times. We have harnessed power to do just about anything we plan to do. But we cannot control a hurricane that can wipe out a city like New Orleans within 30 minutes. No one can determine if this city or other afflicted cities can ever be rebuilt to look beautiful and function again. The power of hurricanes and twisters has not been harnessed and is getting stronger as the years go by. Earthquakes, too, have become very powerful and can quickly destroy just about anything. In the field of health, humankind has succeeded in lengthening our lifetimes by 10-20 years, creating babies with the help of needles and chemicals. But we are not ready to feed the hungry and eliminate poverty so that those people can also live a productive life and feel that they are part of the world. We have a long way to go to solve these problems.

Sometimes people ask me if I have any "plans." My answer is that anyone who is 86 and makes big plans should be careful and be aware that his or her life is, at this point, really in God's hands. Actually, our lives are always in God's hands, but somehow, when we are younger and more robust, perhaps more naïve, we have at least the illusion that we have some kind of control. I feel that all we can do is make good decisions and choices and live life the best way we know how, with reasonable goals and a code of ethics.

Much of my code of ethics came from my parents, who were lucky enough to live into old age. They were good, solid people, who knew how to adapt to the changes that were thrust upon them. Certainly, the life they ended up living was not the one they had envisioned; no Jew would have anticipated having to leave everything they had ever known and relocate to a new, foreign land. But with the help of the good people who shepherded us out of the chaos of Germany, my parents settled into a new life in the Baltimore and remained there until their respective deaths. The photos show them, still a devoted and dignified couple, even as they aged.

* * * * * * * *

It is hard to think about my parents without connecting them to Norbert Lehman, to whom they owe their lives. I am grateful beyond measure for his efforts, and grateful, too, that his son, John Lehmann, is in touch with my family.

Only recently an email came in from John to my daughter Deborah. In it, John expresses the ongoing emotions we both have for his father – respect and awe. And so Norbert's legacy is carried on.

* * * * * * * *

When I think about the greatest satisfaction I have had in life, my thoughts immediately and consistently turn to my children and grandchildren. Life has not really been about adventures, surviving a war, or creating a business. It has been about relationships with people, about contributing to the lives of other people, and caring about those closest to me. A good family life is the greatest accomplishment anyone can have, and I can say that when I look at

Memories Inbox

☆ Marilyn Lehmann More options Jul 22(5 days ago)

Hi Deborah,

How do you do?
Just to touch base for the time being. We are about to go on vacation and I am taking 'Armageddon' with me for some light reading. I will contact you with more questions when I return.
In the meantime please convey to your father my respect and thanks. He is very important to me because, with the exception of my Aunt Bertha, he is the only adult who knew my father when he was a comparatively young man. My memories of my father were in his last few years when he was already very ill. I never had an opportunity to have an adult appreciation of him.
Werner has added a whole new perspective of his life and character, and has explained and answered a number of questions that I had in my mind, for instance, I did not know to what extent he was involved in helping people to escape from Germany. I am only now discovering that he was part of a network of people in London and New York, and this explains why his contemporaries held him in such high esteem.

With kind regards

John Lehmann

Reply Forward Invite Marilyn to Gmail

my two daughters and their families, I have had a positive role in this accomplishment.

I am still healthy enough to enjoy life and to keep on playing a part in the lives of people who are important to me. I am not asking God what I am still doing here at this age! I just enjoy every day and feel I should still do the best I can with the time that I have. It is still a joy to grow my vegetables out back in the garden, to harvest them and share them with friends and family. It is still always a pleasure to attend a happy occasion, a graduation or wedding of someone dear to me. It fills me with happiness to see the young people in my family going forward and succeeding in their ambitions. I choose to spend every day in the most positive and uplifting way; I feel this is the obligation I have, having been given the gift of a long and healthy life. And in fact, even just the process of putting the whole story together and telling it has been life-renewing. And so I shall continue to experience life this way, until I am called to a better place.

I have one small document that seems to encapsulate the very feelings I have about the way I have lived my life. It is a letter that came to me in November, 2005, during the last stages of constructing this memoir. It comes from Manfred Rommel, the son of General Irwin Rommel, who served as Mayor of Stuttgart in the 1990s.

Mr. Rommel and I had met at a reception in his office in Stuttgart in 1993. The photo records this special event.

Then I wrote to him in 2004 to invite him to the D-Day commemoration in Normandy, but he was not able to attend. Then after that, I wrote him once again, just to say hello and see how he was doing. This is his response, and I feel that Mr. Rommel's letter speaks for itself:

MANFRED ROMMEL
Eduard Steinle Strassse 60, 70619 Stuttgart

November 27, 2005

Dear Mr. Kleeman,

Many thanks for your letter of November 23, 2005, which I found after a long stay in the hospital. My Parkinson's disease has gotten worse, and so that is why I must, with some difficulty, use the computer to write to you. I am sorry to hear that you endured such a difficult storm during the crossing. The Normandy invasion was a strategic master achievement and a historic turning point. You are right to be proud of your contribution to it.

With many good greetings,
Manfred Rommel

In June of the following year, I sent Mr. Rommel a copy of Gatling's diary and a draft manuscript of this memoir. I had known during my life in the 4th Infantry Division, that the colonel was keeping a notebook. I felt that he was an outstanding scholar for doing this. But he had always refused to share the information in this diary, and it was information that I felt many people would value.

While he was alive, I'd visit him and regularly remind him about those notebooks, but I could not persuade him to transcribe them for anyone

MANFRED ROMMEL

Eduard Steinle Straße 60
70619 Stuttgart

27. November 2005

Mr. Werner Kleeman
45-46 196th Place
Flushing New York 11358
USA

Lieber Herr Kleeman,

haben Sie vielen Dank für Ihren Brief vom 23.11.2005,den ich nach einem längeren Krankenhaus vorfand. Mein Parkinson ist wieder stärker geworden. Deshalb kann ich auch auf dem PC nur mit Mühe schreiben. Es tut mir leid, daß Sie von dem Unwetter so schwer getroffen wurden. Die Landung in der Normandie war eine strategische Meisterleistung und ein weltgeschichtlicher Wendepunkt. Sie sind zu recht stolz auf Ihren Beitrag.

Mit vielen Grüßen

Manfred Rommel

else to see. When he passed away, I told his son and daughter that they must unearth these books, and unearth them they did! They found them stored in the trunk in Gatling's basement, and they themselves went to work at transcribing them, even though some of the military titles were hard for them to decipher. They did an excellent job of bringing these accounts back to life. What they came out with was a transcript of their father's personal notes about his army life, which lasted more than six years.

Seeing that I was keen to get my hands on as many precious documents as possible, Gatling's children also showered me with all the history books from their father's personal library as well as his D-Day map, which was, by then, a very valuable document.

They gave me permission to disseminate copies of the diary, and so I sent transcripts to the libraries at West Point, the Army War College, and Carlisle Barracks in Pennsylvania. They were most grateful for these materials.

I was delighted, soon after sending these same materials to Mr. Rommel, to receive back this little note:

MANFRED ROMEL

Eduard Steinle Strassse 60
70619 Stuttgart

July 12, 2006

Dear Mr. Kleeman,

Many thanks for your letter and good luck for your book project. I will ...... your description of D Day 2004/1944 and I mention it sometimes in my speeches.

God bless you.

Manfred Rommel

Then only a few weeks later, to my utter delight and surprise, I received a package from Rommel containing an excerpt from his own book, <u>Future and Past</u>. From the enclosed note I learned that he had quoted a letter of mine in the text.

ROMMEL
EDUARD-STEINLE-STRASSE 60
70619 STUTTGART

12. 7. 2006

Dear Mr. Kleeman,

Many thanks for your letter and good luck for your book project. I will read your description of D Day 2004/1944 and I mention it sometimes in my speeches.

God bless you

Manfred Rommel

July 30, 2006

Dear Mr. Kleeman,

Many thanks for your letter and the two manuscripts, which I have read with compassion and profit. They deserve indeed to be published. I was so impressed by your letter from 2004 that I quoted it in my last book. I send you a copy of the passage concerned. With my best wishes for you and your family, I remain

Manfred Rommel

The excerpt from the book shows how these war experiences overlap with one another:

In the spirit of reinventing the peaceful acclimation, the German Bundes Chancellor was invited to attend the ceremonies memorializing the invasion of Normandy, 2004. A short time after this celebration, a former German who was thrown out of Germany in 1939 for being a Jew and became a citizen of the USA wrote a letter to me. On June 6, 1944, as an American soldier in the United States 4th Infantry Division, he landed in Normandy.

After 60 years, on June 6, 2004, he visited the former battlefields with friends and families. The daughters dangled their legs in the Channel and said, "This water is not so cold..." But it had been very cold 60 years ago. When I was up to my neck in it! On Sunday, June

Manfred Rommel
30.7.2006

Dear Mr. Kleeman,

many thanks for your letter and the two manuscripts, which I have read with compassion and profit. They are deserve indeed to be published. I was so impressed by your letter from 2004 that I quoted it in my last book. I send you a copy of the passage concerned. With my best wishes for you and your family I remain

yours

Manfred Rommel

(My handwriting gets worse and worse because of Parkinsons disease)

6, 2004 we stayed at the hotel, being overtired, and refused to be stranded in highway traffic. This was a very smart move for us because most people could not move or travel in any direction. Everything was closed to traffic. The French are unable to regulate traffic.

This letter impressed me. In it, a very understanding human being was able to explain how he overcame great injustice. The defeat that we Germans suffered during 1944 offered us a new chance for freedom and to accept this unusual opportunity. With all the accusations in the world today, my feelings of gratitude will not be relinquished, since this would negate everything we have accomplished....

I suppose that if every participant in the war survived to tell his or her own story, we would all see pieces of ourselves in each other's work. In this sense, we are all one community, a community that had a common experience lived from various perspectives.

I am, as I have said throughout this memoir, honored to have been a part of that community, and grateful for my life as an American. When I receive correspondence such as Mr. Rommel's, I know I am in good company.
Werner Kleeman, September, 2006

Addendum: Books to which I have made contributions:

1959 - *The Longest Day*, Cornelius Ryan. This is the history of the D-Day preparations the landings, the people. I was interviewed by the author over the phone. (Ultimately made into a movie, which is regularly aired on TV on significant dates.)

1984 – After Roberta Oster "found" me, NBC invited me to participate in its documentary "D-Day Plus Forty Years." I was honored to join Tom Brokaw in Normandy, where the filming took place. My daughter, Susan Elgart, attended the program with me. It was aired on June 6, 1984, on national television.

Is Paris Burning? I was interviewed by phone about the experience of entering Paris on that famous day, August 25, 1944, in which the city was liberated. (Ultimately made into a movie, which is regularly aired on TV on significant dates.) We Paris veterans were invited to a private showing in a theater downtown the night before the film was released. I was there with John Keenan, among others.

The Lehman Family, by Dr. Roland Flade, Dr.

Ursula Gehring Münzel. My daughter, Suan Elgart, contributed to the translation of this book into English. I donated a copy to Lehman Brothers, where Theodore Roosevelt IV is a director. Mr. Roosevelt is the grandson of the late Brigadier General Theodore Roosevelt Jr., who was an officer with the 4th Infantry Division in England and France during WWII.

1988 - *History of the Jews of Gaukönigshofen*, by Dr. Thomas Michel, University of Bamberg, Germany. I contributed my own information and experience to this work. When citizens of Gaukönigshofen refused to supply Dr. Michel with any information, he contacted me and asked for help. I met with him in the village and took him to various eyewitnesses who, at my behest, opened up and related their experiences during *Kristallnacht*. They also offered some photographs of people who had been sent to death camps and never returned.

1995 - *Philip Hart: The Conscience of the Senate*, by Michael O'Brian. I made various contributions to this book. Philip Hart spent his entire army life with the 4th Infantry Division, where he achieved the rank of Colonel before being discharged. With the input of Hart's personal friend, Major Lewis

Fiset, I supplied the author with some of the information on Hart's life. The Senate office building is named after Hart, which is a great honor, especially when it is achieved within one's lifetime.

2004 - *History of Brigadier General Theodore Roosevelt, Jr.*, by Robert Walker. I was interviewed for this book, which was published in 2006. Major Fiset and I contributed to the work, which discusses how Roosevelt was the first officer to land in France on D-Day, and later received the Congressional Medal of Honor for this heroic deed.

2004 – I sent a complete set of the proclamations which the US Army had posted, after the war, to the Leo Baeck Institute. Leo Baeck is the largest collection of German and Nazi history, specifically the destruction of European Jewish life, property and culture under the Nazi regime. We survivors have an obligation to record our memories for future generations of researchers. One should never forget the criminal acts of a government which brought about the annihilation of millions of people, just to suit its own philosophies.

2005 - A story of the death camp survivors who

returned home after liberation, by Leila Levinson, published in 2006. Major Fiset and I were interviewed by the author, who is a professor at the University of Texas, Austin.

2005 - *Armageddon*, by Max Hastings. The author was a British war correspondent. I was interviewed for two and a half hours, in person, by the author. Hastings interviewed soldiers from both the Allied forces and the Russian army. He describes in detail the dramatic, final days before the German army collapsed and surrendered.

2006 - Untitled documentary about Brigadier General Theodore Roosevelt, Jr., by Doug Stebelton, produced and released in 2006. This covers Roosevelt's life and accomplishments during WWII. Included are the history of the war, pictures and text about the 8th Infantry Regiment, D-Day in France, Belgium, Luxembourg and Germany. I donated a copy to the Roosevelt Museum in Oyster Bay.

2006 - *From Dachau to D-Day*, the story of my life, written with the assistance of Elizabeth Uhlig, published in 2007. Additional contributions by daughter. Susan Elgart.